ANTIQUE ORIENTAL RUGS AND CARPETS

Philip Bamborough

Antique
Oriental Rugs
and Carpets

photographed by
David Couling

**SPRING
BOOKS**

First published in Great Britain in 1979 by
Blandford Press Ltd.

This edition published in 1989 by Spring Books
An imprint of Octopus Publishing Group plc
Michelin House
81 Fulham Road
London SW3 6RB

ISBN 0 600 56619 6

Produced by Mandarin Offset
Printed and bound in Hong Kong

2063.OC-4   00   000002658   0510   00172

Title page illustration: *19th century Daghestan rug.*

Contents

Acknowledgements

The author and publishers would like to extend their grateful thanks to the numerous people who have lent their whole-hearted support in the preparation of this volume.

In particular, thanks are due to Mr J. L. Arditti of J. L. Arditti Carpets, 88 Bargates, Christchurch, Dorset, for his generous help in making available the carpets and a large number of the rugs illustrated in this book, and for liaising with a number of private collectors who have lent their rugs and carpets for photography.

Thanks are also due to Messrs. Christie's, London, The Victoria and Albert Museum, London, and the Origination Picture and Photo Library, Bournemouth, for providing and granting permission to use illustrations reproduced in this book.

Foreword

The world of oriental rugs and carpets is extremely complex, and to those with little or no experience, seems like a complete mystery. In this book I have tried to remove some of this mystery, to present in a matter-of-fact way the background to the subject and the basic facts on the numerous kinds of rugs and carpets, which will enable those interested to be able to identify rugs and ascribe them to their centre of origin. I hope the book will be of use to the collector as well as to those simply interested in one of the world's greatest art forms.

I have not attempted to give hints on buying and acquiring rugs, for there really is no substitute for experience; therefore if one does not have experience, it is best to go to someone who does, i.e. a reputable dealer. One word of warning, however; beware of cheap rugs – a good rug will always find its correct price level. Whilst on the subject of experience, one must remember that book knowledge alone is only half the picture – to complete it, practical experience is necessary in handling and seeing as many specimens as possible; only then will the true meaning of this book become apparent.

FRANCE

Venice

Pisa

ITALY

SPAIN

PORTUGAL

Madrid
Manises
Valencia
Alicante
Cordoba
Granada
Almera
Malaga

Fez

GREECE

BLACK SEA

Edirne
Istanbul
Isnik   Ankara
Bursa
Bergama   Divrigi
ANATOLIA
Konya
Kuba

Palermo

SICILY

Tunis
Qairawan
Mahdia

MEDITERRANEAN SEA

Tripoli

NORTH AFRICA

Marrakesh

SYRIA

Aleppo
Qasr al - Hayr
Ra

Damascus
Khirbat al - Mafjar

Jerusalem

Cairo

EGYPT

R. Nile

Me

M

RED S.

Tercan

Tabriz

iyarbekir

Maraghah

Mosul

CASPIAN SEA

Gunbad-i Qabus

Amol

Meshed

Teheran

Nishapur

Rayy

Saveh

Veramin

uphrates

Hatra

Sultanabad

Kashan

IRAN

Samarra

R. Tigris

Baghdad

Isfahan

IRAQ

Ukhaydir

Kufa

Shiraz

PERSIAN GULF

ARABIA

TRANSOXIANA

R. Oxus

Samarkand

Bukhara

Kesh

CHINA

Turfan

Herat

Kabul

AFGHANISTAN

TIBET

R. Indus

Delhi

Tughlakbad

R. Ganges

PAKISTAN

Agra

Fatehpur Sikri

INDIA

ARABIAN SEA

SRI LANKA

One of the world's most famous carpets, the Ardebil carpet, made in Persia and dated 1540.

Introduction to Oriental Rugs

What exactly are oriental rugs or carpets and why are they so much sought after and cherished? This seems an obvious question to ask before going into great details about the many varieties. Fortunately it is not difficult to answer. When people speak of oriental rugs and carpets they generally mean the hand-knotted pile rugs, made by village and nomadic craftsmen and women in Iran, Turkey, the Caucasus, Turkmenistan, Afghanistan, etc. The term, however, also encompasses non-pile rugs and carpets such as the kelims and the hand-knotted rugs of India, Tibet and China. The range is vast.

The appeal of the oriental rug lies in its individuality, in its combination of subtle colours and design and in the fine craftsmanship, which places it above a simple floor or wall covering and into the field of art. The finest rugs are normally antique, though the term is used loosely to indicate rugs and carpets of age. Modern rugs are still made in the traditional manner, and some are of high quality, but this book deals mainly with the antique.

The origin of hand-knotted rugs is lost in the mist of time. Archaeologists and historians have uncovered evidence to show that the techniques and even some of the designs used are extremely old. It has been suggested that the tradition originated in the tents of the nomads of Central Asia. Evidence to support this was discovered by Russian archaeologists, who in 1947–9 uncovered a tomb in the Pazyryk Valley in the Altai Range in southern Siberia. This tomb proved to be extremely important, for not long after the burial, water had seeped into the tomb. The result was that the entire contents became frozen and preserved. When carefully excavated and melted, a superb woollen rug was found almost perfectly preserved. Excavation also revealed that the tomb had been robbed, but fortunately the robbers had paid no attention to the rug. Now known as the Altai or Pazyryk Rug and carefully kept in the Hermitage Museum in Leningrad, it measures some 6′ × 6′ 6″ (1·8 × 2 metres). Although the colours have slightly altered over the years the design is clearly visible. Although the tomb was of a Scythian chief, the archaeologist who discovered it thought it to be Persian. However, some years later he found further examples of knotted carpets in another tomb that seemed to prove otherwise. Close examination of the rug also reveals other clues to its Scythian origin. Whoever made the Pazyryk Rug, it is of superb workmanship – a fact that indicates the tradition of rug weaving was already well established at this time. The design itself is of interest for it uses motifs reminiscent of those found on rugs some two thousand years later.

The centre of the rug is composed of a rectangle of squares arranged in four rows. In

One of the oldest known rugs, the Pazyryk Rug, about 2400 years old, found in 1947/9 in southern Siberia.

all there are twenty four squares; in the centre of each is a cross like that of St. Andrew and very similar to that used on Sejur rugs. Around this central rectangle of squares are bands of elks and mounted horsemen, each band separated by either griffons or St. Andrew's crosses. The knots are well executed, about two hundred and seventy to the square inch. Thousands of years, however, separate this rug from the Islamic rugs of today.

For the oriental rug is, if not the most famous, certainly the most popular of Islamic arts. It is at once symbolic of the Orient and such rugs have found a place in the houses and great collections of the world. Today they are sought after, collected and used by connoisseurs and interior decorators and by those who buy them simply as a means of financial investment.

As works of art the rugs and carpets of the nomadic tribes and of the village workshops are perhaps the most perfect expression of the Islamic ideal of art, the infinite pattern. A true art of Islam they reflect the life and culture of the peoples of the Islamic world from the earliest times, for rugs and carpets were an essential element of Islamic interior decoration, both of the tent and of the building. They embody all forms of Islamic art, geometric, figurative, floral and arabesque.

Not all oriental rugs and carpets are Islamic in origin, however, for fine and important floor coverings were made in China and Tibet, both of which have their own traditions. Some too were made by Christian Armenians. However separated into their own particular spheres, they can be seen as an integrated and overall tradition, as the entire area of the Middle East, Central Asia, the Caucasus, Tibet, India and China was linked by a maze of trade routes, which were themselves lines of cultural communication. Thus, however remote and indirect, some interconnection can be argued for all forms of oriental rugs.

Carpet weaving in Islamic countries is a traditional craft and is extremely old. Continuous evidence of development from early specimens does not exist, but fragments of early rugs have been uncovered in Egypt at Fustat, one of which can be dated to the year 821. There is also reliable evidence to suggest that fine carpets were produced under the Seljuks. In spite of these early manufacturing traditions, what can be termed the golden age of the Islamic rug did not begin until the 16th century. Before this early period another separate tradition can be attributed to Egypt.

The Egyptian tradition, pre-Islamic in origin, utilised a beautiful colour combination of a ground of burgundy red with the design worked in green and light blue. The design which was divided into sections was principally geometric in form, usually consisting of primary motifs of stylised papyrus plants, rolled leaves and secondary motifs of arabesques and interlaced ornaments. The entire area of the rug was taken up with motifs and because of the absence of contrast between the field and the border, there appears to be little difference between the two. The fall of the Mamluk dynasty in 1517 also marked the end of the true Egyptian tradition of rug weaving, for the downfall of the dynasty heralded the introduction of Ottoman ideas displacing the old. At first there was a fusion of Mamluk and Ottoman ideas, but later Ottoman ideas became entirely dominant.

The most beautiful and the most famous Islamic rugs are those of Persia, Turkey and the Caucasus. There is little documented history of the earliest Persian carpets and actual specimens are just as scarce. The reason for the scarcity of early specimens lies in the perishable nature of the carpets and rugs and in the fact that they were made to be used and thus subject to wear and deterioration. Great care was taken of rugs and carpets, for they were greatly cherished and valued by all who owned them. In spite of this, age and wear knows no barriers and many fine specimens have disappeared forever.

The vulnerability of rugs and carpets due to the ravages of time is clearly illustrated by the date of the earliest specimens that have survived to the present day. For, although carpets appear to have been made in Persia over a thousand years ago, the earliest complete specimens that have survived appear only to date to the end of the 15th/16th centuries.

An extremely beautiful and valuable specimen, not only from the artistic but also from the historic point of view, is the famous Ardebil carpet, now in the Victoria and Albert Museum, London. This superb carpet, which helps give us a datable anchor, is dated to the Islamic year (AH) 947 which is equivalent to A.D. 1540. It was made by order of Shah Tahmasp between 1539–40 by Maksud al Kashani for the Shaykh Safi Shrine in Ardebil. The carpet, which measures 37′8″ × 17′5″ (11·5 × 5·3 metres) is woven in beautiful but sombre colours in an elaborate floral design. The large central medallion appears to be the underside of a typical Safavid dome of a mosque with two mosque lamps hanging, one to the right and one to the left, attempting an illusion of perspective. Originally there were two carpets, but one was sacrificed in order to repair and restore the other one. The remains of the other are in the Los Angeles County Museum.

Persian carpets vary enormously in size, ranging from those such as the massive Ardebil carpet to diminutive prayer rugs measuring a little over a metre or yard in length. In shape they are normally elongated and rectangular rather than square. The colouring is deep and rich with the ground normally being indigo or crimson. Rich warm yellows, browns and greens were occasionally used, while yellow, although common, has faded and appears today mostly as a neutral tint.

The common material for both rugs and carpets was wool; warps and weft could be of wool or cotton according to circumstance. A very special form of rug employed a silk pile in place of wool and some of these are much sought after. Even rarer are carpets incorporating gold and silver thread in the pile. Persian silk pile carpets were very popular in Poland in the late 16th and early 17th centuries. These imported treasures from Persia are strangely called Polish carpets.

In early Persian rugs and carpets, that is those made before the 18th century, it is extremely difficult if not sometimes impossible, unless the piece has a recorded pedigree, to attribute them to their town or village of origin. Classification of old Persian carpets is more commonly made according to the style or design, for example 'animal', 'vase', 'garden', 'floral', or 'medallion'. Only later does it become possible to attribute them to specific towns such as Senneh, Feraghan, Isfahan, Kashan, Shiraz or Tabriz. They are however easily distinguishable from Turkish or Caucasian rugs by virtue of their distinctive designs and colours, weaving patterns and in most cases by the knot. The Ghiordes or Turkish knot which is symmetrical was used in Turkey, the Caucasus and a few other adjacent countries, while Persian weavers tended to favour the Senneh or Persian knot which is non-symmetrical.

The majority of Persian carpet designs are based on floral motifs with occasional figurative designs, both human and animal, as well as a few simple geometric ones. 'Garden' carpets are laid out either in the form of a plan of a garden, with paths, flowerbeds, ponds, etc. or more generally clumps of flowers and plants. The age of the carpet or rug will determine whether or not the floral arrangements are placed in regular networks. In the 17th century, the blossoms are large and conventional and the stems form an intricate network, while in the 18th century the tendril network becomes even more elaborate, with the blossoms becoming rosettes. Animal carpets portray among other subjects hunting scenes, while medallion rugs and carpets base their design on a large central medallion with lobed outline, similar to that used on the

Ardebil carpet. The so-called vase carpets are simply a formalised variety of floral carpet which contain the outlines of vases. Although it is generally difficult to attribute pre-18th century rugs and carpets to any particular centre, there is a rule-of-thumb that may be applied which will give a reasonable chance that a carpet may come from a particular area. Generally speaking the 'animal' carpets may be said to have been made at Isfahan, 'vase' carpets at Joshaqan, while the large medallion carpets were developed at Herat.

A quite different yet great tradition of rug weaving developed in Turkey. Early Turkish rugs still followed Seljuk inspiration utilising angular patterns but were soon replaced by designs of stylised animals and birds. The 'animal' carpets of Turkey are, however, quite different from those of Persia in that they show a strong Turkish element. The oldest known Turkish Ottoman rug bears the date 1584. It was probably made at Ushak.

The regions associated with Turkish rug and carpet making, Ushak, Ghiordes, Bergama, Kula, Kirshehir and Ladik each had their own individual designs and colour schemes. The rugs from Ushak, for example, are known for their wonderful 'star' designs. Rows of large stars filled with abstract arabesques or flowers are worked in yellow or white on a deep blue base, surrounded by a white outline contrasting with the superb Anatolian red ground of the carpet. It is a Turkish cousin of the Persian medallion pattern.

The Turkish rug industry was a peasant occupation of the countryside, rather than in factories under the direct patronage of a sultan. Large carpets were not as popular in Turkey as they were in Persia. Rugs were made with the same materials as the Persian, wool with the occasional use of cotton for warps and wefts, and for special rugs – silk. Designs are often called by nick-names or trade names. The so-called 'Holbein carpets', the 'classical' Turkish rugs, have designs or rows of staggered polygons formed of interlaced arabesques. Another popular design is the so-called 'bird' design which, although it has the appearance of birds, is in fact floral.

In addition to the Turkish and Persian traditions, there are two other Islamic rug and carpet weaving groups. They are the Caucasian and the Turkoman. The rugs and carpets of both of these groups are principally the product of nomadic tribes. They are generally unsophisticated yet have a charm and quality which place them amongst the best oriental carpets. Rugs tend to be medium and small in size with designs being severely geometric.

A final expression of the Islamic genius of rug and carpet weaving appeared in India. The carpets of this great sub-continent were based originally on Persian models but soon developed a typical style of their own to suit the tastes of the Moghul emperors. The colours are distinctive and are generally not favoured elsewhere in the Islamic world. Carpets commonly break with the tradition of abstract and continuous floral patterns, which were replaced with superb pictorial representations, monumental expressions of miniature paintings. There is little doubt that the pictorial rug which was first developed in Safavid Persia blossomed into a fully developed art in Moghul India.

The rugs and carpets of China and Tibet come from an entirely different background, though those of Tibet share a common nomadic craftsmanship with some of the rugs of the Caucasus and Turkmenistan. Even some of the Chinese rugs made in the border regions share this nomadic heritage. However, the classical Chinese carpet is something quite different. For although recent archaeological discoveries in China indicate that rug making is an extremely ancient art, having perhaps a common ancestor with the other branches of rug weaving, Chinese rugs and carpets are principally the product of well organised 'factories'. They are also extremely conservative, drawing their artistic inspiration from indigenous sources such as Buddhism and Taoism.

Turkish wool pile rug on woollen warps. 16th century.

Weaves and Weavers—The Main Groups

PERSIAN

Abadeh, Afshar, Ardebil*, Bakhitiari, Bijar, Feraghan, Malayer, Hamadan-Mazlaghan-Lilihan-Mushkabad, Mahal, Mehriban*, Mosul*, Isfahan, Joshaqan*, Karaj*, Kashan, Kerman, Khorasan, Meshed-Birjand, Mir*, Mud, Nain*, Qashqa'i*, Qum, Sarab, Saruq, Senneh, Seraband*, Shiraz, Tabriz, Tehran, Heriz, Veramin*, Yezd*.
*Rugs marked * are not described and illustrated in colour but are described in the section 'Other Rug Making Centres'.*

The general label 'Persian' is probably the one most commonly applied to oriental carpets and rugs. As a geographical label, however, it is in some respects vague for its borders have varied from time to time. The name Iran was bestowed upon the country in 1935 by Reza Shah, however, when describing geographical areas of origin of rugs or carpets it is more usual to use the old name, Persia.

Rugs and carpets have always been cherished in Persia where they have been an important part of the interior furnishing of house, palace or tent. Rugs and carpets were found in the homes of the rich and the not so rich – only the quality would differ. There is an old Persian saying 'The richer the man the thinner the carpet' (i.e. the better quality). Carpets of Persian origin have been traded both inside and outside Persia for centuries. They are a commodity for investment both to Persians as well as to others; indeed they are often regarded as a better investment than conventional stocks and shares. At one time every important household had its own weaving workshop, where the weavers would make rugs not only for domestic use but also for accumulating a surplus, for rugs and carpets were considered better than money and were even used for paying taxes!

Rugs and carpets have been made in most parts of Persia; the list of some of the kinds of Persian rugs described in this book is itself formidable. Some centres are, of course, more famous for their rugs and carpets than others, some are simply market towns which have given their name to the rugs that pass through them. The more sophisticated and certainly the larger carpets are the product of urban 'factories' made under the direction of a master weaver, while others, mainly small rugs, unsophisticated yet charming in conception, are the work of nomadic tribes such as the Qashqa'i.

It is not unusual even in modern day Iran to see the entire floor covered by rugs and carpets. There is, in fact, a formal and traditional way of arranging rugs, which has the great advantage that the floor coverings can be adapted for use in any room, whether large or small. There is normally a central rug, the Mian Farsh, which may be anything up to 18 feet (5·5 metres) long and 8′ 3″ (2·52 metres) wide. At one end running cross-ways is the principal rug or Kellegi which may be nearly 12 feet (3·6 metres) in length and up to 6 feet (1·8 metres) wide. Either side of the Mian Farsh and running up to the Kellegi are the Kenarehs – about the same length as the Mian Farsh but only about 3 feet (0·9 metres) wide. The majority of early Persian rugs are fairly narrow and long; this is not only due to the average shape of rooms but more to the fact that a large number were made on the narrow looms of the nomads.

Apart from use in homes, carpets played an important part in the festive decorations of court and public occasions. They also were used to great effect as the sumptuous floor coverings of mosques and by the faithful as prayer mats. The latter were made in most centres. They play an important part in the life of a faithful Moslem, who is expected to pray five times a day, in that the rugs protect the worshipper from the dirt when he kneels down and touches his head on the ground, facing all the time towards Mecca. Prayer rugs are small in size and have a central mihrab – a representation of the prayer-niche which indicates the direction of Mecca in mosques.

A look at a map of Iran will show how widely distributed are the centres of rug-making. In the north-west, Iran borders Turkey and the Caucasus, now part of the Soviet Union – in this area are Karabagh, Heriz, Tabriz, Gorevan, Mehriban, Sarab, Azerbaijan and Ardebil. To the west on the Iraqi facing side of Iran is Senneh, the centre which gave its name to the Persian knot. In this area too are the Kurdistan nomads, while the Luristan nomads are in the south-west, as are the Qashqa'i and Bakhtiari nomads. In the south are the centres of Shiraz, Fars, and to the east Kerman; the Afshar nomads are also in the south. To the east is the territory of the Baluchi nomads, while north-east the area is inhabited by the Tekke and Kurdish nomads. Between them is Meshed. The other major centres such as Feraghan, Saruq, Qum, Kashan, Khorasan, Mahal, Mir, Isfahan and Abadeh are situated in the large central area of the country.

TURKOMAN

Turkmenistan – Uzbekistan – Afghanistan – Yomud – Salor – Bukhara – Beshir – Pendiq – Baluchi.

For the purpose of discussion the Turkoman group can include Afghan and Baluchi rugs, for they all have one thing in common – colour. The majority of the rugs and carpets from these areas have red as a predominant colour. Shades vary, however, from deep red, wine, scarlet to pale red – the common dye being obtained from the madder root. They were, and still are, made in a large area spanning more than one country – for the rugs are the work of nomads.

Turkoman rugs are made by Turkoman tribes which are spread over an area including Turkmenistan (Turkestan), now a Soviet republic; the Soviet Republic of Uzbekistan; Afghanistan; and some by the Tekke tribe which about thirty years ago left Turkmenistan and now live in the northern steppes of Iran. The tribes traditionally have been nomadic sheep-rearers, living where possible in suitable pasture lands. They are horsemen and fierce warriors, for in days gone by they fought for pasture and water, supplementing their income by raiding caravans and travellers. Being nomads they respected no land, and no frontiers.

The rugs are made by the women on the horizontal or ground loom which is portable but primitive. It also imposes a restriction on size; thus nomad rugs are seldom very large. Most out-put was intended for domestic use and consisted of rugs for the tent (or hut), saddle-cloths, camel-bags, door hangings, wall-hangings as well as storage bags such as the hanging torba and the juval. Surplus production was marketed at the market towns such as Bukhara, Meshed, Herat etc. Fine quality rugs were also made specifically for sale. Today, in those areas of the Soviet Union which the Turkoman tribes inhabit, they have been encouraged to become 'settled' and many rugs are now produced in workshops and marketed through State agencies. However, in spite of the fact that the pattern and quality of the material remain much the same, the general appearance and appeal of the modern rug is nowhere near the same as its 'wild' ancestor. Design is almost invariably based on the octagonal 'gul' of which there are several distinctive varieties.

Woven in the same region by Turkoman nomads are the Beshir rugs – these too are predominantly red but yellow and green are also found. Afghan rugs at first glance also appear similar to Turkoman, but a second examination will separate them, for there are a number of differences. Originally woven by Turkoman nomads, they are today almost exclusively the work of the Afghans. Apart from differences in technique, design and colour variations, the knotting is coarser and the pile longer in comparison. Baluchi rugs have somewhat uncertain origins, for although made by Baluchi tribesmen they could come from Iran, Afghanistan or the vague area in the border regions. Baluchistan itself, often accredited with the manufacture, is a somewhat uncertain candidate for the honour, for the dozen or so Baluchi tribes, each with its own pattern preference, are scattered – Meshed for instance in Iran was one of the principal centres for marketing Baluchi rugs.

CAUCASIAN

Chi Chi – Kuba – Daghestan – Derbend   Karabagh – Kazak – Shirvan – Sumac.

The Caucasus have been at various times home to many different peoples including Turks, Armenians, Persians and the nomad tribes of Central Asia. All have enhanced its rich heritage of rugs. For although from many different races, the resultant Caucasian rugs have a distinctive quality, which is easily discernible whether they come from north or south.

The rugs come from a difficult and generally inaccessible mountain area between the Caspian and Black Sea. At one time under the control of Persia, it came under Russian domination in 1813. Today it is part of the Soviet Union. The rugs come from centres in the southern part of the country, from Derbend, on the western shore of the Caspian Sea in Daghestan, south of Derbend, from Kuba, Chi Chi, and Sumac, and south-east from the village of Shirvan, also situated near the shore of the Caspian Sea in southern Azerbaijan. To the west is the home of the Karabagh rugs, while north-west of the Karabagh region in the mountainous heart of the Caucasus, is the home of the Kazak rug.

Caucasian rugs have the distinctive feature of being severely geometric. Every subject has been made geometrical, even human figures, animals, birds and flowers; all are composed of arrangements of straight lines. In addition stars, swastikas and rectangles are also used to great effect. Colours are blue, red, yellow, ivory and green. Mostly of wool, the rugs are all knotted with the symmetrical Ghiordes or Turkish knot. Caucasian are among the most popular of oriental rugs.

ANATOLIAN (Turkish)

Bergama, Ghiordes, Isparta, Kayseri, Kirshehir, Kula, Ladik, Milas, Mudjur, Koum Ka Pour, Panderma, Sivas, Smyrna, Ushak, Yahyali, Yuruk.

Anatolia is the old name for Turkey – in the rug world it is still used to describe Turkish rugs. The Anatolian rug has been known in Europe longer than its cousin from Persia. So high was their reputation that in the 16th century Cardinal Wolsey ordered sixty of them. In fact, until the early 17th century, to the European the oriental rug was Anatolian, and it had a noticeable influence on the evolution of designs and patterns of European and Spanish carpets. So identified with the craft of hand-knotting was it, that until the 18th century, hand-knotted pile upholstery was known as turkey-work. In the 19th century, literally thousands of rugs were exported to Europe. Known as Smyrna carpets (Izmir) after their collection and export centre on the coast, these carpets are notable for their light background and floral decoration in green and pink.

The rugs and carpets come from all over Turkey, from the shores of the Mediterranean to the interior. They are noticeably different from the Persian rug, both in concept and in weaving technique; the main colours are red and blue, and designs generally avoid the depiction of men and even animals, for being Sunnites they observed the Koranic law (which forbade this) more strictly than the Persians, who were Shiites.

Anatolian prayer rugs are bright, yet at the same time have an air of religious sobriety about them. They are sometimes woven in green, a sacred colour.

Some of the rugs show other influences such as Caucasian and Persian. Another odd fact is that some were made by Christian Greeks who had settled in Turkey and to all appearances were in fact Turkish. Many of these left the country when Ataturk established the modern state of Turkey in 1922.

INDO-PERSIAN

India (Agra-Lahore etc.), Pakistan, Kashmir.

Generally speaking Indian rugs and carpets can be said to be in the Persian tradition. Having said this we must immediately seemingly contradict this statement by adding that they are also distinctly Indian. The reasons lie both in the history of carpet making in India and in the geography of the sub-continent.

Early Indian floor coverings were made from pressed and matted wool. These 'Nandis' or what we now call 'Namdas' are recorded in a document of the eighth century. Pile rugs were not introduced into India until about 1580 when the Moghul emperor Akbar established a royal workshop in his palace and brought weavers from Persia to work in it. Some of the carpets from their workshop have become world famous. One is in the Girdlers' Company in London, another is in the Victoria & Albert Museum, London. Jehangir, Akbar's son, continued the Royal patronage as did his son Shah Jehan. Carpet factories were set up at Lahore, Agra and Delhi.

The original designs were Persian, inspired by Kerman, Kashan, Isfahan, Herat etc. After a while, Indian weavers took up the craft and workshops were established under the patronage of wealthy merchants and noblemen. It was in these workshops that variations in design began, by adjusting designs to the individual requirements of the patrons. The Indians' love of nature, of animals, birds, flowers and trees, so beautifully expressed in Indian miniature painting, soon found its expression on carpets.

Beautiful floral carpets were made, while others with animal designs were full of life and energy. Designs leant towards the pictorial. Colours too changed. They became lighter than the Persian with a distinctive use of pink.

The Indian carpet continued to be admired and cherished both within and without its country of origin. In 1851 the 'industry' received a major boost at the Great Exhibition at Crystal Palace in London. This in a way marked the end of individualism, for to meet demand, carpet 'factories' were established at Mirzapur, Amritsar and in Kashmir at Srinagar. With demand increasing rapidly quality fell equally rapidly, however, the situation eventually steadied.

Kashmir is particularly noted for its fine carpets and rugs, but as a centre it has had its ups and downs. It is said that carpets were first woven in Kashmir in the mid 15th century, in workshops established by Prince Shahi Khan who had his interest in rugs aroused after spending seven years in Turkestan. After his death, the industry declined, until it was revived in the 17th century by Ahmed Beg Khan, a governor of Kashmir. The industry continued but it was not until the 19th century that Kashmir carpets really created interest. Based on the Persian model, the Kashmir carpet has continued the tradition but has also introduced some Central Asian designs. Unlike Persia, the weaving is done by men and small boys.

Pakistan can perhaps be considered in the sphere of influence of the mainstream rug producing countries, being bordered on one side by Afghanistan and Iran and by India and Kashmir to the east. It is, however, only a secondary centre, the industry having been introduced in the 16th century at Lahore. The rugs are in the Persian style though rugs in Caucasian and Turkoman designs have also been made. They are similar to Kashmir rugs but generally inferior in quality, though the older specimens are of very high quality indeed.

CHINA

The rugs and carpets of China are in complete contrast to those of the Islamic world. Very little detail is known about the various centres of rug production or about individual periods. What is known, however, enables us to understand the background of a rug and to estimate its age. Carpets, in China, were woven in organised workshops or factories. They were not, except for a few small rugs made on China's northern and western borders, made by nomads.

In comparison to the Islamic rugs these are formal, but only in a conservative way. That is that the rug had been completely conceived and formalised before weaving began. It also means that as with most Chinese arts and crafts, designs tended to be conservative and to be used in later periods; thus they are generally of little value in assessing a carpet's place of origin or period.

Chinese rugs vary somewhat in quality from the rather crude, made with a mixture of coarse and ordinary grade wool, to really magnificent pieces. In some carpets from eastern China, the weft and warp is sometimes of cotton, while in west China, north China, Manchuria and Chinese Turkestan the weft and warp tends to be in wool. The Senneh or Persian knot is used. In silk rugs, weft, warp and pile are of silk, though on certain cheaper varieties warps may be of cotton.

Styles can best be attributed to those which developed under the patronage or which received the favour of certain emperors or dynasties, such as Ming, K'ang-hsi, Ch'ien Lung etc., but attributing a carpet with say a Ch'ien Lung design does not attribute it to the period, for like all Chinese art, archaic designs were often reproduced in reverence of the period. Designs are generally Buddhist or Taoist in inspiration.

During the Ming dynasty, an unusual rug was woven in which the pile stood in relief against a background of gold and silver threads. Ming styles were generally 'pre-Persian' in inspiration; colours tend to be subdued and sombre. In the reign of K'ang Hsi, however, Persian influence showed itself, while Ming designs were also copied. Further influences from abroad including Turkestan, East India, Central Asia and Manchuria expressed themselves in the Ch'ien Lung period. It must be remembered that the Ch'ing dynasty, to which both K'ang Hsi and Ch'ien Lung belonged, was Manchu in origin and not indigenous Chinese.

In spite of all these outside influences, Chinese rugs are instantly identifiable from corresponding Persian, Turkish or Central Asian examples. The colour range of the Chinese is far more limited than the Persian. Primary red is rare in China, while apricot, peach, blues and yellow were greatly favoured. Natural wools were also popular. Green is generally not found in rugs earlier than the Ch'ien Lung period, and is rare before 1875.

TIBET

Tibet – Ladakh – Sikkim – Bhutan – Nepal.

Tibetan rugs are not sophisticated but are the products of nomads and small villages. They are small in size and usually extremely colourful, if not gaudy. In design they are similar in some respects to the Chinese but with strong Central Asian and Mongolian artistic overtones. The symbolism is Buddhist.

Made of rather coarse wool and thickly knotted, they come in various shapes, suitable for use in tents or small huts or houses and include horse trappings such as saddle-cloths. They are not over strong, and when compared to the nomad rugs of Islamic countries appear distinctly crude.

It is not possible to attribute rugs to any particular part of Tibet or with any certainty to any period. Also made in small villages, the craft has extended to those areas of the Himalayas on the Indian side of the Tibetan border including Ladakh, Sikkim, Bhutan and Nepal. Tibetan refugees in India are continuing the craft, but the designs are no longer traditional.

Shapes and Sizes

Each region and indeed each centre has its own particular range of rug shapes and sizes. Some are quite varied while others are restrictive. The detailed description given of each centre later in the book indicates the common range of sizes one might expect to come across for that centre. The following, however, is a list of names in common use in the rug world which are used to describe various shapes and sizes.

Ak Joli Turkoman decorative horse blanket.

At Joli Turkoman horse blanket.

'Baby' Rug, about 2′ × 4′ (0·60 × 1·20 m). See *Namaseh*.

Cherlik Turkoman, saddle cloth.

Dip Khali Turkoman, small carpet used at the threshold of a tent.

Dozar A large rug measuring between about 6′ 6″ × 4′ 6″ (2·00 × 1·40 m) and 6′ × 4′ (1·83 × 1·22 m). The name is derived from 'do' meaning two and 'zar' a measurement. See *Zar*.

Engsi Turkoman door hanging, i.e. a rug intended to be hung as a door flap over the entrance of a tent or hut. These are often decorated with a hatchli design.

Herek Small rug measuring about 4′ × 2′ (1·20 × 0·60 m).

Jolam A thin, narrow strip measuring anything up to 60′ (18 m) long and 6″ to 2′ (15–61 cm) wide. Originally intended as hut decoration, but finds other uses in European homes.

Juval Bag face commonly associated with Turkoman tribes. The name appears to be Turkish in origin and is used to describe bags or bag faces. They measure from about 3′ 3″ × 6′ 6″ (1·00 × 2·00 m) down to 2′ 7″ × 5′ 3″ (0·80 × 1·60 m).

Kellegi Persian term describing the head rug of a set. They are normally two to three times as long as they are wide, generally about 5′ 6″ × 11′ (1·67 × 3·35 m upwards to 6′ × 16′ 4″ (1·83 × 5·00 m).

Kenareh The Persian name Kenareh used to describe the side runners in a formal arrangement of rugs actually means 'sea shore'. Two Kenarehs run either side of the main central rug the 'Mian Farsh' and the Kellegi (see above) is laid across the end of the arrangement. The Kenareh can be anything in length from 16′ (4·88 m) to 25′ (7·62 m) and are about 3′ 4″ (1 m) wide or thereabouts.

Makatlik The Turkish name for a runner.

Mian Farsh The main central rug in a Persian formal rug arrangement. See *Kellegi* and *Kenareh*.

Namaseh Originally a small easily carried prayer rug. As they were all of similar size the word has been adopted to describe any rug whose dimensions are about 2′ × 4′ (0·61 × 1·22 m). See *'Baby'*.

Pendjerelik A rug similar in purpose to the Engsi in that it was intended to be hung over the entrance of a tent. However, it is noticeably different in that it is as long as a small size rug but only about 18″ (·45 m) to 20″ (·62 m) deep with a thick long woollen fringe which can be around 4 feet in length (1·20 m). The fringe is intended to keep insects and heat out but let light in.

Pushti A small pile bag or cushion. It is also applied as a dimensional term to small rugs or mats of about 2′ × 3′ (61 × 98 cm).

Qali Persian and Turkish name for a rug also written Khali and Kali. As a description of rug size it is normally taken to apply to rugs measuring 6′ × 10′ (1·80 × 2·80 m).

Sejadeh A dimensional term for a rug of about 4′ × 7′ (1·22 × 2·13 m).

Torba Turkoman bag measuring about 2′ 6″ × 4′ (0·8 × 1·2 m). These hanging bags were used inside the Turkoman nomads' tents and used for storage. See also *Juval*.

Ukuki Turkoman, bag used for binding over the ends of the yurt (tent) poles when the nomads were on the move.

Yastik The Turkish name for a very small rug which may range in size between 10″–15″ (0·25–0·40 m) in width to 20″–30″ (0·50–0·80 m) in length. Said to be originally a prayer hassock. Also used for sitting on.

Yatak A sleeping rug with long pile. The word is Turkish for 'bed'.

Zar A Persian unit of area, the exact area of which varies from centre to centre. Generally it is about 13·5 to 16·5 square feet (1·20 to 1·50 square metres). It sometimes is also applied to a width of about 1 metre.

Zarand A Persian dimensional term named after a town north of Kerman. About 4′ 6″ × 2′ 3″ (1·38 × 0·69 m).

Zarcharak A Persian dimensional term applied to rugs measuring about 4′ × 2′ 8″ (1·22 × 0·81 m).

Zaronim A Persian dimensional term applied to rugs measuring about 5′ × 3′ 3″ (1·52 × 1·00 m). Persian word for 1½ Zars. See *Zar*.

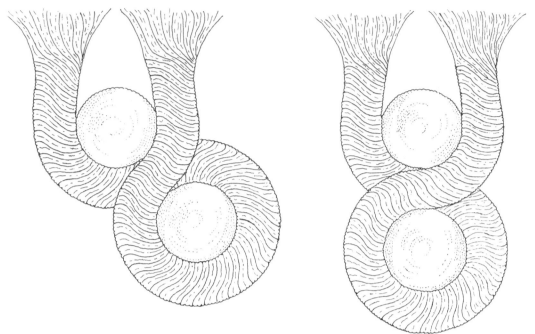

Two versions of the asymmetrical Persian Senneh knot.

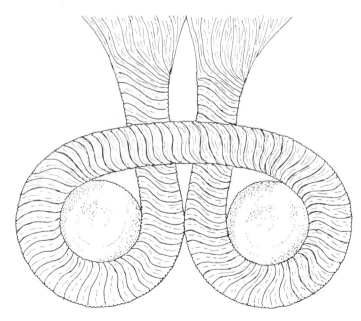

The symmetrical Turkish Ghiordes knot.

Materials and Techniques

All oriental rugs, with the exception of kelims and Sumacs which are weft faced, have a hand-knotted pile. They consist principally of three main parts, the warp, the weft and the pile. All were made on looms, however primitive or sophisticated, using either wool, cotton or silk, either separately or in combinations. The weft and warp may be left natural or dyed, as can the wool or silk of the pile, which in the best rugs is always dyed with natural dyes.

WOOL

This is principally sheeps wool, though goats hair, lambs wool, camel and yak hair are also sometimes used, depending on the centre of manufacture of the rugs. Long strand wool is the best, as it makes for a finer and stronger pile. On a sheep, wool from the flank and shoulder is preferable to that which comes from the legs and stomach. Quality wool comes from fleece combed in the winter or shorn in the spring. In Persia, the finest wool is said to come from Khorasan. Generally, sheep in cold areas such as the mountainous regions give superior wool to those that graze in the warm valleys and plains. Wool from lambs between eight and fourteen months old is of the highest quality. Although its quality varies enormously wool is still an excellent material for rug making, and some of the finest and most exquisite oriental rugs are made either partly or wholly from it. Many nomad rugs are composed almost entirely of wool. The Luri and Kurd tribes supplied, in addition to their own needs, spare wool from which many of the carpets in western Persia were made.

The sheep must first be sheared or combed, after which the wool is carded, washed and spun. Spinning was and is normally a primitive process, carried out by hand. Although slow, it is the most suitable for making rugs – being more loosely spun than machine spinning, it also tends to take the dye better.

COTTON

Cotton is grown and hand spun in Persia and India, and in fact in most of the countries which make hand-knotted rugs. With the exception of the Kayseri rugs of Turkey, where it is used with the same effect as silk for knotting white motifs and for highlighting others, it is used exclusively for warp and weft. As stated above, wool is in some cases also used for warp and weft, but those rugs with a cotton foundation are generally more durable. They do not stretch or distort in the same manner as some rugs with woollen warp and weft, and on the whole, rugs with cotton foundations seem to lie better on the floor.

SILK

Silk has been used for weaving some of the finest and lightest of carpets. As well as a silk pile, some rugs also have silk warp and weft threads. A really superb silk carpet has to be seen to be believed; one such, a Koum Ka Pour, is illustrated on page 115. Silk comes from the cocoons of the silk worm which needs mulberry trees to feed on; thus silk can only be manufactured where a supply of these trees is on hand to feed the worms. Most of the silk used in Islamic rugs comes from China. Some silk is today manufactured in Kashmir, where it is used in textiles and special rugs.

DYES

The dye is all important to the production of a good rug; for it affects both the colour and condition. A bad dye can make the pile dry and brittle. It is therefore not surprising that someone who knew the intricacies and secrets of dyeing was highly regarded in rug-making circles.

Dyes used in the majority of hand made carpets and rugs are all natural, derived in the main from plants and insects. The most common colour, red, was derived from several sources, from the roots of a three to six year old madder plant, *rubia tinctorium*, which grows wild in many parts of Persia; from cochineal, extracted from the bodies of the female *Coccus cacti* insect, this gives a shade of carmine red; and *Chermes abietis* from which a different shade is obtained. Various shades of red, especially shades of pink were obtained by mixing the red with whey.

Blue was obtained from the leaves of the indigo plant, which grows in the East Indies. A particularly dark hue was obtained from the encrustation which formed on the inside of the fermentation vats. Browns and greys were produced by either using natural undyed wool, or by treating it in solutions obtained from ox-blood. Black was a particularly difficult colour to dye as, if the process was not properly carried out, the fibres would become brittle and eventually break away from the pile, leaving a strange sort of relief effect. This was always a danger when a dark coloured natural wool such as grey had to be used. The best blacks were natural, from black sheep or camels.

To obtain yellow the dyers used either the flowers, leaves and stalk of the reseda plant, the stems of pomegranates (orange) or vine leaves, or more rarely as it became very expensive, the dried pistils and pollen of the saffron crocus, which gave a distinctive saffron yellow. Greens were made by mixing yellow and blue.

The success of dyeing with natural materials depends very much on the skill and the knowledge of the dyer. For varying conditions and materials often meant that it was extremely difficult to control the colour, quality, texture and brilliance of the wool. Water also played no small part in influencing the outcome of the dyeing process. Results depended a great deal on the relative hardness of the water. A problem with natural dyes is that it is difficult, if not impossible, to obtain identical shades of the same colour. In town or village workshops, this difficulty was overcome by dyeing in a vat at one time the total amount of wool of a particular colour needed for a rug. Nomads who were constantly on the move could not, however, do this, as the facilities required simply could not be portable. They had to resort instead to dyeing the wool as and when required in small containers. This had the result that varying shades of the same colour were used in the same rug, a feature which has added to the attraction of nomad rugs, as the overall effect of design and colour variation is very pleasing. This variation, however, cannot be achieved deliberately, for the result would appear stiff and artificial. This discrepancy of colour is known as abrash.

Complete stability of colour and shade was offered by the introduction of aniline dyes in the early 1860's. In the beginning, this was achieved at a price, for there were many side effects. The early aniline dyes, although quickly welcomed by the rug-making centres of Persia and Turkey, proved unsuitable for rug yarns, for they were brash and harsh, and tended to fade rapidly. The reputation of the rug-making centres faded with the dyes. The result was chaotic, traditional export markets ceased to order. To the Persian government, this switch to aniline dyes was alarming, for it had only been made on economic grounds as it was generally quicker and cheaper to use aniline dyes. The result was that the government intervened and banned the use of these dyes, introducing severe penalties for all who ignored the order. Thus, while the carpet makers of non-Persian countries often resorted to aniline dyes, Persian rugs during the same period (1903–1914) were made using the traditional natural dyed yarn. This point must be borne in mind when assessing the age of a Persian rug.

After about 1920, the quality of synthetic dyes increased dramatically, and today synthetic dyes are produced in a range of colours and shades with a quality that should satisfy even the most discerning eye. With the advance of synthetic dyes has also come changes in the dyer's art, for he is now able to tone-down the synthetic colours to make them look paler and more antique, by treating the rug in a reduction wash. This somewhat tricky operation does not harm the rug in any way, if carried out correctly.

The process of dyeing, whether by nomad or town workshop, is basically the same in principle. Firstly the wool is soaked for about thirty minutes in hot water, and then immersed in an alum bath for up to twelve hours. After this it is boiled for an hour in alum-water before being placed in the dye vat, where it remains for a period from just a few hours to a number of days, depending on the colour and nature of the dye-stuff. The alum bath helps to ensure that the dye will be fast. Even though the wool is all dyed at one time it may still have colour variations, due to differences between the wool of individual sheep. Dyeing silk is even more difficult and requires all the skills of a master dyer.

Before leaving the subject of dyes and colours, we should remember that like designs and patterns, individual colours have a symbolism and special meaning, depending upon the centre or country of origin of the rug or carpet. First and foremost, green was regarded as a sacred colour in Islamic countries, as it was supposed to have been the colour of the prophet Mohammed's coat. Until the 1930's in Persia it was banned for use as the ground colour. Its use was, however, allowed on prayer rugs or in minor amounts in the secondary motifs of rugs. Pressure from export markets, however, helped to overcome this reservation. Green is symbolic of spring and the annual cycle. The following is a brief list of colour symbolism:

White The colour of mourning, death and grief (*Persia, India and China*). Also symbolic of peace and purity.

Black Destruction (*Islam*).

Orange Devotion, piety (*Islam*).

Yellow Imperial colour (*China*).

Red Joy, happiness, wealth (*Islam, China*).

Light Blue Power, symbolic of power (*Mongolia*). Symbolic of heaven (*Persia*). National colour of Persia, also associated with mourning.

Dark blue Solitude.

Brown Fertility, agricultural abundance (*Islam*).

Gold Power, wealth (*Persia*).

There are sometimes a number of different meanings for the same colours.

LOOMS

There are basically two kinds of looms – horizontal and vertical. The horizontal loom is a nomad loom and is of the simplest possible construction. It is narrow and relatively easy to transport, hence its use by the nomads. Consisting simply of two beams or rods from which the warp threads are strung, lengthways, from one beam to the other. The whole assembly is pegged down by posts driven into the ground, which hold the beams and warp threads taut on the ground. When not in use, the rug, plus loom, can be rolled up for transport. It can be carried with little difficulty on the back of a mule or camel. Its limitation however is size; thus all nomad rugs are small in size. There are a number of variations of this type of loom, one of which is illustrated on page 125.

There are three types of vertical looms – the fixed vertical, the roller beam vertical and the Tabriz vertical. Vertical looms are used in small village workshops and in the larger town 'factories'.

The simplest of the three is the plain vertical loom. It is used mainly in villages and small workshops. It consists of two vertical supports from which two horizontal parallel beams are fixed, one at the top and one at the base. Between these rounded beams the warp threads are stretched. A ladder or pegged rung is affixed to each vertical support pole of the loom. Between these a plank is attached on which the weaver or weavers sit. As the warps are fixed, and cannot be raised or lowered on rollers, the weavers must move with the weave, starting at floor level and moving upwards, rung by rung, until sometimes they reach the ceiling. The weavers always work at the same height as the knots. Carpets made on such looms are normally the same length as the loom, though of course they can be less. The maximum height for this type of loom is normally about nine feet (2·74 m). It is possible to make longer carpets on a vertical loom, by using a double length of warp that is wound round one of the beams. This is repositioned after the first length has been completed, by winding up the knotted rug and unwinding the warp, but the result is normally unsatisfactory and detectable in the finished product.

A variation of the fixed vertical is the Tabriz loom. Invented by weavers in that town, it is now used in other parts of Iran. The basic difference is that the warps run down one side and up the other in a loop. After the front warp has been worked, it is slipped under the lower beam and up the back, which allows the back warps to ride over the top beam and down the front ready to be worked.

The final development is the roller beam vertical. In this type, the warp is rolled on the upper beam and stretched to the lower beam. Both beams are on rollers. The weavers sit at the base of the loom and wind the knotted rug around the bottom beam when finished, at the same time unravelling fresh warp from the top beam. Carpets of any length can be made on this type of loom. A roller beam vertical loom is illustrated on page 165.

THE WARP

Together with the weft it forms the foundation of the rug. It is the name given to the threads which stretch lengthways between the beams of the loom, whether horizontal or vertical. In nomad rugs the warp is wool, while in others it can be of cotton or more rarely of silk. The surplus warp at each end of the rug or carpet forms the fringe.

THE WEFT

The weft is the thread that is woven in and out across the warp between rows of knots. Varying between one to three or four rows, depending on the centre of manufacture, its purpose is to hold the knots firmly in place. The threads of the weft are pushed firmly against the knots by being beaten with a comb-beater.

THE KNOTS

There are two knots common to hand-knotted rugs, whether Persian, Turkish, Turkoman, Caucasian, Indian, Tibetan or Chinese. They are the Ghiordes and Senneh – the former named after a town in Turkey and the latter after a town in Persia. They are also referred to simply as the Turkish or Persian knot. A strange fact is that although the Persian knot is named after the town of Senneh, the majority of rugs from that town are made with the Ghiordes knot! As a general rule, however, Turkish rugs are made with the Ghiordes and Persian with the Senneh. The Ghiordes is also used in the Caucasus and by the Turkoman tribes. In the detailed description of rugs later in the book, the Ghiordes or Turkish knot is indicated by the following symbol:–

It is symmetrical and is formed by looping the woollen yarn around two adjacent threads and drawn up between them in the manner illustrated in the diagram on page 26.

The Senneh or Persian knot is indicated in the detailed descriptions later in the book by the following symbol:—

$$\int_\omega$$

The knot is asymmetrical and is formed by looping the pile yarn under one warp and over and under the adjacent warp, the ends pulled upwards, one end between each warp.

By examining the pile of the carpet (brushing sideways) and scrutinising the back, it is possible to identify the knot used, the nature of the warp, and the weave pattern, i.e. the relationship of the wefts to the knots. This examination can give valuable clues to the experienced eye as to the origin and age of a rug.

PRODUCTION

Nomad rugs are principally made by women (and children) as are some of the rugs of small village workshops. However, the larger workshops employ a master weaver or salim, who may have a number of female and male weavers in his charge. Children are also employed as they have small nimble fingers. In India and Kashmir, weaving is principally a man's work (as well as that of children). Women and children generally have slimmer and more subtle hands and can work finer carpets by knotting finer and denser knots. They may also have more patience, though this is simply conjecture.

There may be from one to five weavers, according to the size of the rug. Even nomad rugs may be worked by more than one person, for example by several women, sometimes with children. It would not be unusual for the average weaver to tie up to 12,000 knots a day. Depending upon the complexity, a range of between 10,000 to 15,000 knots is possible; a nomad woman weaver will produce rather less, in the region of 6,000–10,000. In spite of this seemingly astronomical figure, a really good rug with a high density of say 250 knots per square inch will take months to produce. The growth of a quality carpet is very slow, and really cannot be hurried. Low density rugs do not take as long, and they usually have larger pile to conceal the looseness of the weave. Another short-cut is the use of the jufti knot. This is a double knot that is formed by knotting around double warps. It has the effect of increasing speed but reducing density. Motifs tend to be less distinct and clear cut where jufti knots have been used. It will be obvious that high density carpets are expensive, simply by virtue of the time taken to make them.

A rug or carpet contains millions of knots, each one individually tied. A kaliedoscope of colour and texture, a wonder of man's dexterity and ingenuity, as well as a testimony to the artistry of the individual weavers. For although a carpet is the result of individual labour and imagination, it is also the product of the collective artistic heritage of a people – a reflection of their aspirations and beliefs. However we must not romanticise for the work is hard and exacting.

METHOD

The weaver starts the rug by weaving a kelim selvedge. This is always at the lower edge of the rug and is worked simply by weaving weft threads in and out of the warp with no addition of knots. The selvedge has the function of forming a firm edge-band against which the first row of knots can be made. It prevents the rug from fraying, keeping the knots tight and the rug together. The selvedge varies in depth according to the centre of production and size of rug.

The pile is begun by tying knots around each pair of warp threads, either symmetrically or asymmetrically depending upon whether the Ghiordes or Senneh knot is being used. Each knot is tied and then pulled sharply downwards. The wool for knotting on horizontal looms is kept in balls in front of the weavers, while in the case of vertical looms it is normally hung in balls from the top of the loom. The weaver takes a length of between $5\frac{1}{2}$–6 inches (14·0 to 15·2 cm) per knot. The knots in Persian carpets are always pulled in a downwards direction and the ends, which are about $2\frac{3}{4}$ inches (7 cm) long at this stage, left. They are not usually trimmed until about six rows have been completed, then they are given a preliminary trimming. The main trimming, a very skilled task, is normally undertaken by a specialist worker, though in nomad rugs this job too will be done by the weavers. This operation can make or break a rug. The amount a rug is trimmed depends upon its density and the requirement of the market for which it is made. Fine, dense carpets are always closely trimmed. Nomad rugs have a thick pile.

KELIMS

Not all rugs are pile rugs for there are also kelims – and Sumacs (see under Sumac). The kelim has its design formed by weaving coloured threads in and out of the wefts, forming a tapestry-like effect. These weft threads never go completely across the rug but return upwards forming lines of block colour, which makes kelims potentially weak in some areas. This division between the weft threads is, however, hardly visible, as they are beaten very tightly together with the warps. Sometimes the threads are hooked around each other. The kelim is, however, not a true rug as in the East – it is used not for floor coverings, but as wall hangings, and bed covers.

An 18th century Ghiordes prayer rug, the central motif being a mihrab arch supported on columns, in a carnation pattern border.

Designs and Patterns

Oriental rugs have many features which make them attractive, but without doubt one of the most important is the seemingly infinite variety of designs. This is achieved by the ingenuity of the weavers, who mix various combinations of traditional motifs and patterns to produce rugs each with an identity of its own. These motifs have developed over many years and are the traditional property of an individual tribe or centre. However, it would be a mistake to assume that they were the exclusive property of a tribe or centre, for motifs were frequently borrowed, adapted or copied. Once adopted and modified, the resultant motif or pattern may again inspire another artistic idea.

The various motifs that have evolved are in a way like a kind of language, because in many cases they have symbolic meanings. They also indicate the area from which the rug may have originated though, as stated above, attribution simply on design may be misleading. Nevertheless, on the whole designs do generally indicate the area from which they come. In the following list of designs that are found on rugs, the centres or tribes which use the motifs are listed together with the area of origin and other areas which have adopted or adapted the motif in their own rugs. It must be remembered that there are many variations, interpretations and innovations of motifs and those illustrated and described here only give selected examples to indicate general appearance. Names too vary, so it may be possible to read two seemingly different descriptions of the same carpet. In the appendix is a selection of photographs with technical descriptions of their designs, composed of motifs some of which are illustrated in the diagrams and some of which are illustrated only in the photographs.

Designs can be divided into two main groups, geometric and curvilinear, i.e. floral or animal motifs. The oldest tradition is the geometric and is fairly widespread, in that geometric motifs are employed on Caucasian, Anatolian, Baluchi, Turkoman, Afghan, and even on some Iranian rugs. Geometric designs are also copied in Pakistan and Kashmir. Designs tend to be natural subjects highly stylised geometrically or simply abstract geometric shapes, the common denominator being that the design is composed of vertical, diagonal or horizontal lines. The best of the designs are improvised by nomadic weavers and not planned in detail.

Curvilinear or floral designs are much younger, not appearing till the early 16th century. They were developed to cater for the taste of the Safavid rulers, reaching the pinnacle during the early 18th century. Rugs using these designs belong to the classical tradition of Islamic art. Designs were developed by ustads or master designers, unlike nomadic designs which were the traditional heritage of a tribe, passed on by word of mouth. The formal Islamic art tradition expressed in floral and curvilinear designs developed local schools of design; thus carpets from different centres have features which help attribute them to those centres. Technical details such as weave pattern are of course important for an accurate attribution to be made and designs must always be studied together with full technical details.

In the following description of motifs, they have been divided into two main groups 1) Those found on Islamic rugs and 2) Those found on Chinese and Tibetan rugs.

Islamic rugs and carpets

FIELD MOTIFS

Afghan guls.

36

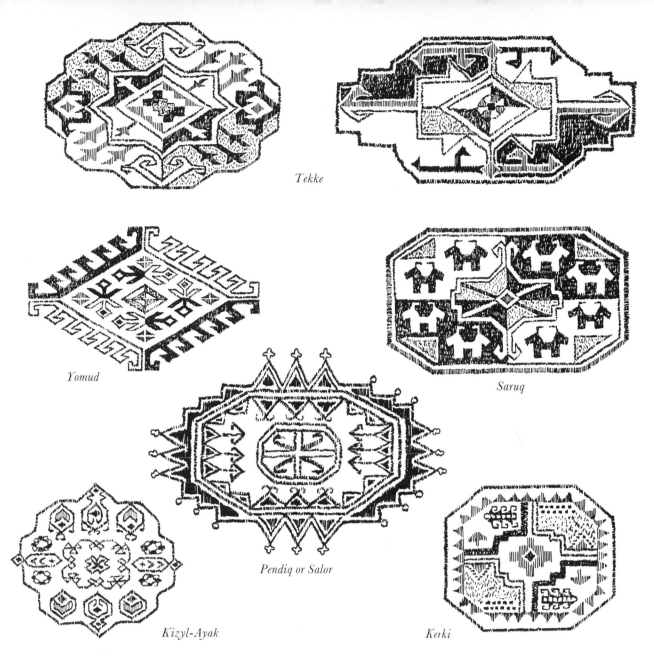

Tekke

Yomud

Saruq

Pendiq or Salor

Kizyl-Ayak

Kerki

The Gul An octagonal motif basic in most Turkoman rugs and carpets. 'Gul' in fact comes from the Persian for 'rose' but must not be confused with 'rosettes' which are described later. It is basically octagonal in form but there are many variations, depending upon where the rug or design originates. The gul is found as the main motif on Bakhara, Afghan, Yomud, Tekke, Chaudor, Saruq and Kerki. It is also copied by a few other centres including Pakistan and India. At one time every Turkoman tribe had its own distinctive gul. Usually on a small rug there may be three guls arranged in a row but in large carpets there may be more than one row.

37

The Boteh This motif is perhaps most familiar as the characteristic Kashmir shawl design. It is known also as the almond motif and as the pine or leaf pattern. Its origin may lie in the shape of the cypress tree. Although it has a number of different variations it is basically an almond shape with the pointed end bent over to one side. It is one of the most frequently used motifs on oriental rugs, being favoured by many centres of rug production. Its centre of origin is not known for certain but some authorities place it in the Seraband region, probably first in Mir rugs for the motif is also knows as Mir-boteh.

In some forms it can be so stylised that it is difficult to recognise. Normally it follows the conventional form of the bent almond. It is not a large motif, being on average about 4 inches (10 cm) from base to tip, and normally covers the entire field of the rug in diagonal or straight lines. The motif has been used by many centres, but perhaps most frequently in Senneh, Kashan, Derbend, Qum, Kerman and Shirvan and of course Seraband and Mir. A few of the many varieties of boteh are illustrated below.

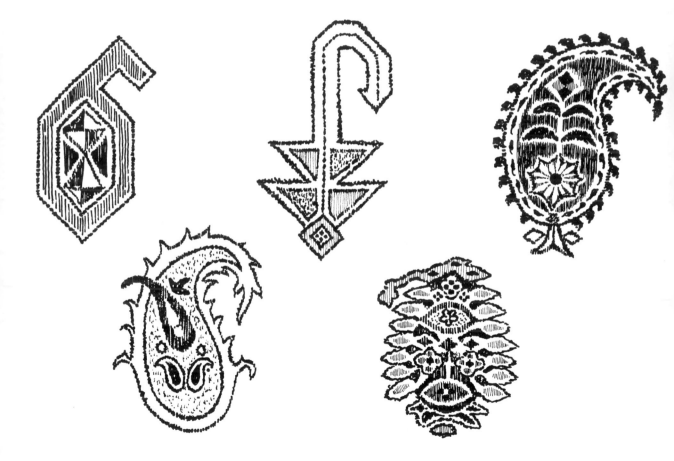

38

Herati In spite of the popularity of the boteh and the widespread use of the gul, the most frequently used design in oriental rugs is the herati. The design, which is named after the city of Herat, originated in Khorasan, yet the motif used there is slightly different. It is particularly favoured in Tabriz, Bijar, Saruq, Kurdistan, Feraghan and Senneh. Some Caucasian rugs also use it. As might be expected, it has been used by a number of centres where it does not constitute the main traditional design.

The basic form of the motif is very simple and easy to recognise; a rosette is enclosed by a diamond on the outside of which four other rosettes or palmettes are placed one at each point of the diamond. Along each side is a curled serrated leaf. In the Khorasan version there is no central rosette in the diamond. The design is normally repeated over the entire central field. Some herati motifs omit the external rosettes or use just two.

39

Mina Khani Like the herati this design also appears to have originated in Khorasan. As an overall field design it is in some ways similar. Floral, it resembles a garden of flowers. A tendril trellis formed by four main flowers is linked to form an oval, which itself is linked together forming a secondary trellis of diamonds. In the centre of the secondary trellis is a rosette from which spring four branches, extending into the ovals in which they blossom. The centre of each oval has a rosette. It is a popular motif on Veramin rugs as well as on Kurdish nomad rugs.

Harshang This motif originated in Persia along with a number of others, during the reign of Shah Abbas. However, it is not common to Persian rugs but to the Caucasian, in particular Shirvan. It resembles a crab, with a central serrated diamond from which extend four stylised claws.

Joshaqan A fairly simple design to recognise. It consists of a field covered with diamond shapes, over which stylised flowers are arranged. There may be a central medallion. It is used on some Kashan rugs but mainly on Joshaqan rugs.

Medallion A design not restricted to any one centre, it is a term of description for medallions, which cover the central field of a carpet and may be floral or geometric, square, circular or rectangular. However, by virtue of the fact that most rugs are elongated, it too is normally longer than its width, in keeping with the proportions. Sometimes smaller medallions or part medallions appear in the corners.

Zel-i-sultan This motif originated in the 19th century, in spite of its name which is taken from a prominent Persian who lived in the mid 18th century. It is easy to recognise in that it takes the form of two vases of flowers, one above the other. The motif may be repeated over the field and sometimes a bird is interspersed sideways between the vases. Sometimes the design consists of single vases rather than double. The motif is common on Abadeh, Veramin and Qum, but is also found on Teheran, Malayer and Feraghan.

Tree of Life A distinctive motif which can occupy the entire central field of a rug and may be pictorial or stylised geometric. There is also a weeping willow pattern generally associated with sorrow.

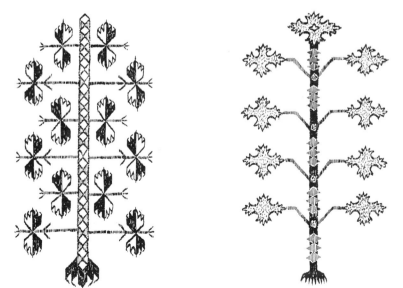

41

Shah Abbas One of a number of designs which originated during the reign of Shah Abbas in the 17th century, it consists of a field covered by rosettes and palmettes, linked together by a trellis of tendrils and branches. It is used by a number of centres, particularly Isfahan.

Seraband In this design the pattern is formed by small palm leaves.

Mir Similar to Seraband but tilting sideways.

Allah Allah A design which is formed by two enclosed inward-facing Seraband patterns, and other motifs. It is repeated over the entire field each side being shared with another.

Arabesque An eight-lobed medallion formed by interlaced tendrils.

Karaj A stylised border and field design from N.W. Persia.

Palmette A common motif employed in various ways in the designs of various rug-making centres. It appears very much as if it is a flower in section. *See also Shah Abbas.*

Rosette A motif frequently found on many oriental carpets. The motif consists of a stylised flower symmetrically arranged as if seen from immediately above.

Star A stylised star-shaped motif, a constituent in many rug designs.

Tarantula A stylised rendering of a large spider, a motif which appears on many Turkoman rugs.

Cypress Tree A constituent motif in design of some rugs.

Mihrab A linear representation of a prayer niche, which appears in a number of forms on prayer rugs. The mihrab is present in all mosques and indicates the direction of Mecca, which all the faithful face when they pray.

Men Geometric representations of humans are found mainly on Caucasian rugs.

Dog Geometric representation found on Caucasian rugs.

Cock Geometric representation found on Caucasian rugs.

Camel Geometric representation found on Caucasian rugs.

Peacock Geometric representation found on Caucasian rugs.

Dove Geometric representation found on Caucasian rugs.

Scorpion Geometric representation found on Caucasian rugs.

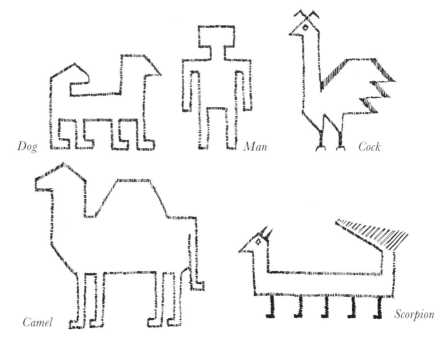

Dog Man Cock

Camel Scorpion

Ram's Horn A motif resembling a ram's horn found on Caucasian rugs, in particular Shirvan.

Hatchli A cross pattern in a rectangle in the centre of the field.

BORDER DESIGNS

In many cases the border of a rug is composed of bands in which variations of the main decorative theme are worked. However, this is not a rule and it is quite possible for the border to be composed of quite different motifs. While the designs of some Caucasian rugs are Persian in inspiration, the borders are always Caucasian.

Boteh Border This border is very similar in appearance to the boteh field motif and is easily recognisable. It can have the same range of stylisation as the field motif but does not appear on its own; rather it is combined with other motifs in a continuous band. The boteh may be large or small.

Herati Border Contrary to what might be expected, the herati border is quite different to the field motif. There are also widely different versions depending upon where the rug or carpet was made. It is used both with field herati motifs and frequently with other central field designs. The border itself is based on a band of continuous rosettes and palmettes, linked by floral motifs. It may be elaborately floral or geometrically severe.

Seraband Border Similar to the Seraband field motif but highly stylised.

Serrated Leaf Border A motif commonly employed on Caucasian rugs, especially Kazak. The design is simple to recognise, in that it appears to be a band of serrated leaves arranged at angles to each other.

Wineglass A border seen in Caucasian rugs, similar to the serrated leaf but one in which the serrated leaves are separated by what looks like a wine glass.

Kufic Border This border design in white which resembles kufic script is found on many Caucasian rugs.

Guards In addition to the main wide borders there are secondary borders which may be similar or different. These narrow borders are called guards. Some of them are associated with particular centres of rug production. A few motifs may also occasionally be found as a wide border.

Diamond Lozenge A guard made up of small bands of lozenges in different colours.

Diagonal Quadrilaterals A guard made of different colours, commonly used on rugs from Feraghan and Shiraz as well as on rugs from some areas of the Caucasus.

Rosette Guard A narrow band of continuous rosettes.

Running Dog A hooked Greek key pattern.

Dog Tooth A serrated negative and positive interlocking balustrade.

Key Pattern Borders of variations of the key pattern are found on rugs from many centres.

'S' Border A continuous band of opposed horizontal 'S' shapes found on Caucasian rugs.

Crab Border A crab-like motif used as a continuous band. Found on Caucasian rugs, especially Kuba.

Some authorities credit these designs with symbolic meanings. Others insist that in the case of Persian workshop-produced carpets the designs were created and used simply because they were beautiful, while in the case of nomad rugs they were inspired by the imagination and the immediate surroundings of the nomad weaver. Whichever is correct, it is true that some of the motifs have known symbolic meanings, which may also have been intended when woven into the rug. Some of the motifs, such as cloud borders in Persian rugs, were inspired from Chinese sources.

Chinese and Tibetan rugs and carpets

The designs, motifs and patterns of China and Tibet are quite different in that they draw their artistic inspiration from, in the case of China, Taoism and Buddhism, and in the case of Tibet, Buddhism only. Unlike the Islamic rugs, there is no uncertainty as to the significance of the design, for nearly every motif has a known symbolism. For the purpose of illustrating some of the motifs these two centres may be discussed together as some designs are common to both.

The Eight Taoist Symbols They are from left to right: the Fan, the Sword, the Gourd, the Castanets, the Flower Basket, the Drum (bamboo tube), the Flute, the Lotus.

The Eight Buddhist Symbols These can appear both stylised and non-stylised. They are from left to right: The Conch Shell, the White Parasol, the Standard, the Two Fishes, the Lotus, the Vase, the Endless Knot, the Wheel.

'Shou' symbols of happiness.

Swastika Not a Nazi symbol but in India, Tibet, China and Japan a symbol of longevity and good things. Appears on its own or as a linked border pattern.

Bat Often appears on carpets. Symbolic of longevity and happiness.

Fish Happy marriage, especially twin fish.

Lotus Symbolic of purity and the Buddha.

Peaches and Peach Blossom Longevity, immortality and 'spring'.

Butterfly Symbol of happiness and conjugal felicity.

Phoenix This bird is thought of by the Chinese as the King of Birds (Feng). The mythical bird is a male symbol and associated with fertility.

Dragon A popular motif on Chinese and Tibetan rugs. A benevolent symbol of power and adaptability.

ATLAS OF ORIENTAL RUGS AND CARPETS

Abadeh

Location of manufacture: Abadeh rugs are named after the village where they are made which lies about 125 miles (201 km) south of Isfahan on the road to Shiraz.

General description: Rug making is a comparatively recent introduction at Abadeh and thus rugs from here have no traditional design heritage. The designs therefore have been drawn from other sources, mainly Iranian though also Caucasian. Qashqa'i influence is also to be seen, derived no doubt from the annual visits of the tribe which camps near the village during the summer.

Basically Abadeh rugs are of two types (though of course a number of designs can be found). The first is a design in which the diamond shaped field has placed within it a central medallion with other medallions being placed (though not always) at the corners outside the diamond. The design can be seen in the illustration opposite. The diamond shape may be the result of Qashqa'i influence, for it is the main decoration of the tribe's rugs. The remainder of the design is composed of small geometric motifs, flower and leaf patterns, recalling those used by the Fars.

The second common design is the so-called zel-i-sultan motif. The design, which is usually comprised of vases of flowers arranged one above the other, covers the entire field. Abadeh rugs are noted for their use of this design, which incidentally is not one of great antiquity. The design is also found on Qum and Veramin rugs. In relation to the field, the borders of the rugs are small, being normally composed of two guards, one on either side of the central band, which is of a different ground to the guards.

Colours are usually harmonious and pleasing and feature flame red, blue, brown, terracotta, and occasionally green.

Specification: *Size* – Rugs usually range proportionally in size from 4′ × 6′ (1·22 × 1·83 m), 6′ 6″ × 9′ 9″ (1·98 × 2·97 m), etc up to 8′ × 11′ (2·44 × 3·35 m). *Loom* – vertical. *Warp* – cotton. *Weft* – cotton. *Pile* – wool. *Knot* – Persian, between 120 – 200 knots to the square inch. The knot is rather large, a factor which causes the zel-i-sultan motif to appear somewhat coarse in relation to other rugs. *Motif* – general Iranian and Caucasian. Geometric and zel-i-sultan.

Description of plate: Abadeh, wool pile, c.1930. 7′ 4″ × 4′ 7″ (2·24 × 1·40 m).

49

Afshar

Location of manufacture: Afshar is the name of a nomadic tribe which inhabits the tableland to the south of Kerman near Shiraz. Today the name of Afshar is also given to rugs made in the villages in the area.

General description: Though originally pure nomadic in inspiration, Afshar rugs share both nomadic and village features, both in their decoration and technical specification. The tribe originally came from Azerbaijan, between the Tigris and Euphrates, but after a dispute with the Turkish sultan, left their homeland for their present location. This happened in the late 16th century. Afshar rugs are made both on the horizontal loom of the nomads and the vertical loom of the villages. Originally the warp and weft were of wool, but today it can be entirely of cotton or a wool weft with cotton warp.

Designs are varied and in addition to traditional Afshar designs include motifs from the repertoire of both the Kerman craftsmen and the Fars tribe. Colours too are varied; cream and white being a distinctive feature – the most common grounds are blue or red.

The motifs can be divided into geometric and floral. Of the geometric designs, the most typical Afshar motif is the so called morgi or chicken design. In this the entire field is covered with what appears to be a repeated geometric chicken design. Another design derived from Shiraz is the large diamond motif, either two or three. The field is tightly covered with smaller motifs, sometimes betraying Kerman floral influence.

Description of plate: Afshar, wool pile, c. 1900. 4' 3" × 4' (1·30 × 1·22 m). Geometric with central medallion and truncated medallions in the corners. Dominant colour blue, both dark and light, with red and yellow.

Also geometric and covering the whole field of the rug is the boteh design known as the dehaj. The influence of Kerman can be seen in the use of floral repetitive motifs, sometimes with a central medallion. Borders tend to be small in proportion to the rug. Common border motives are the diamond chain and the serrated leaf, the latter especially associated with the dehaj design.

Specification: *Size* – Large carpets are not common, the most usual sizes are proportionally – 3′ 6″ × 5′ (1·06 × 1·52 m) and 4′ 6″ × 7′ (1·37 × 2·13 m). *Loom* – vertical and horizontal. *Warp* – wool or cotton. *Weft* – nomad/wool; village/cotton. *Pile* – wool. *Knot* – nomad/Turkish 40 – 150 knots square inch; village/Persian, about 40 – 100 to the square inch. *Motifs* – geometric botehs, the so called morgi or geometric chicken, diamond shapes related to Shiraz and floral motifs influenced by Kerman.

Description of plate: Afshar, wool pile, c.1880. 7′ 10″ × 3′ 6″ (2·39 × 1·07 m). In this rug the effective use of ivory can clearly be seen. Geometric 'tree of life' and floral motifs predominate.

53

Bakhtiari

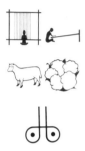

Location of manufacture: The rugs of the nomadic Bakhtiari tribes are made in a region which extends south of Isfahan towards the Persian Gulf. To the north the area is bordered by the Zaindeh River, while on the south and west it is flanked by the Sagros Mountains.

General description: The carpets and rugs of the Bakhtiari are distinctive and easily recognisable by their special designs. The field of the rug is nearly always divided into squares or diamonds or similar shaped sections, each of which contains floral and/or flowering plant motifs and occasionally animals. The design may be repeated in each section or changed using a number of motifs. Although originally nomad in inspiration and execution, today many of the nomads have settled in villages and have absorbed Persian designs and techniques. Thus Bakhtiari rugs and carpets can be found with both Turkish and Persian knots. They also can be made on vertical and horizontal looms.

Some Bakhtiari tribesmen, who have forsaken the nomadic life in favour of more settled conditions, have turned to rug-making for a living. Their rugs, from the village of Shahr Kord show strong traditional Persian influence in contrast to their nomadic tradition. Here the herati border is popular. More traditional borders utilise the serrated leaf pattern. Colours are generally dark; red, green, brown, with highlights in yellow ochre and a vivid blue.

Specification: *Size* – They range in proportion from 5′ × 8′ 9″ (1·52 × 2·67 m) to 5′ 6″ × 10′ 6″ (1·67 × 3·20 m). Large carpets are also known. *Loom* – vertical, though the horizontal loom is also used in some locations. *Warp* – cotton, though occasionally wool is found. *Weft* – cotton or wool; two threads. *Pile* – wool. *Knot* – predominately Turkish, between 80 – 120 knots to the square inch. Carpets exceeding 120 knots per square inch are known; these have only a single thread weft and are of very high quality. The Persian knot is primarily employed at Shahr Kord.

Description of plate: Bakhtiari, wool pile, c.1940. 6′ 6″ × 5′ 1″ (1·98 × 1·55 m). The field is divided into diamond medallions containing floral motifs. The cream background of the border is a distinctive feature found on many of these rugs.

55

Bijar

Location of manufacture: Bijar is a small town in Kurdistan about 30 miles (48 km) from the town of Senneh.

General description: Rugs from Bijar are distinctive technically as well as in their attractive designs and colours. Technically they are distinguished by the fact that they usually have five weft threads composed of two loose wool threads, one taut cotton thread followed by two loose wool threads. These are tightly beaten together against the knots with a special tool, creating an extremely tight and compact rug.

The designs are mainly floral, Persian classical, though less sophisticated than rugs from the classical Persian centres. They are extremely charming and attractive. The herati motif is common, repeated to cover the entire field. Central medallions are also common. Occasionally the medallion is found on a self-coloured field – here the four corners have floral motifs. The borders are small in relation to the size of the carpet and may be composed of as many as eight bands. The wide main border often has the boteh motif, while stylised floral motifs are common on the guards. The border herati motif is also found.

Colour is very effectively used, with the decorative motif standing out against a dark background of blue, red or green. Turquoise as a design colour is used strikingly. Bijar rugs are extremely strong and long-lasting.

Specification: *Size* – most shapes, the commonest sizes range in proportion from 4′ × 6′ 6″ (1·22 × 1·98 m) to 6′ 6″ × 11 ft (1·98 × 3·35 m). *Loom* – vertical. *Warp* – cotton, occasionally wool. *Weft* – combination of cotton and wool – five strands; 2 wool, 1 cotton and 2 wool. *Knot* – Turkish, between 100 and 200 knots to the square inch. *Pile* – wool, hand spun. *Motifs* – traditional.

Description of plate: Bijar, wool pile, c. 1860. 6′ 7″ × 4′ 9″ (2·01 × 1·45 m).

56

Feraghan

Location of manufacture: Feraghan carpets and rugs from Mushkabad in the district of Feraghan, which lies between the town of Saruq and Arak. Mushkabad was destroyed in the 19th century and thus true Feraghan carpets, with the exception of a few that are made in the village of Ibrahimabad, are no longer made. They are of high quality. A coarse rug from the district is exported and marketed under the name Mahal.

General description: The herati motif in one form or other is commonly found on Feraghan carpets; it often covers the entire field. Another popular device is the central medallion, which is covered with the herati motif but stands apart from the rest of the field by virtue of its different background colour.

Common colour combinations are dark red or blue for the main field with the medallion in lighter blue or white. Blue and red are the dominant colours, with yellow, white, and green providing the highlights.

Sometimes the central medallion is replaced by a pair of medallions. The zel-i-sultan motif is also found both in the field and the border.

The border is interesting in that it often combines geometric designs on the outer guards with boteh motifs or stylised flowers on the inner guards. The main border may also be decorated with border herati. The entire border gives the appearance of a number of closely decorated bands.

Specification: *Size* – ranges in proportion from about 5′ × 10′ (1·52 × 3·05 m) to 8′ × 20′ (2·44 × 6·10 m). *Loom* – vertical. *Warp* – cotton. *Weft* – cotton. *Pile* – wool, close cropped. *Knot* – mainly Persian, 80 – 160 knots per square inch.

Description of plate: Feraghan, wool pile, late 19th century. 6′ 4″ × 4′ 4″ (1·93 × 1·32 m).

58

59

Hamadan

Location of manufacture: The city of Hamadan, perhaps the most important centre of rug-making in Iran, is situated in the north-west of the Iranian plateau. The term Hamadan, however, is applied to rugs from a wide area around the town.

General description: Hamadan was once the capital of Persia during the period of the Seljuks and is today the catchment centre for rugs from numerous towns and villages, many of which have been weaving rugs for centuries. Because Hamadan rugs are drawn from such a wide area, they can be extremely varied in design. They are very hard wearing and generally of good quality, but lack a spark of inspiration. Rugs are also made in the town, but this is a fairly recent development. The Hamadan group itself includes Lilihan, Mahal, Mazlaghan and Mushkabad rugs. Of the main area near the town the best rugs come from the village of Khamseh to the north of the town and Borchelu to the east. Apart from the village rugs, Hamadan also encompasses some nomad work that is brought into the town for sale. The term Mosul is sometimes applied to rugs of the Hamadan group, though this is incorrect and misleading. Rugs so-called are generally not of high quality, the knots are not close and the woollen pile somewhat coarse. It thus can be sometimes used to distinguish high quality Hamadan from lesser quality.

Khamseh rugs are normally distinguished by their central medallion of geometric form. The corners are decorated with a similar design to the central medallion and the border, normally three banded, displays highly stylised motifs.

The herati design is perhaps the most common motif used on the rugs from Borchelu. A red background is favoured. Sometimes a floral or geometric medallion on an ivory background is found. As with Khamseh rugs, the design of the central medallion is repeated at the corners. The central border repeats the main design, while the two flanking guards tend to display a continuous rosette design. Generally speaking a natural camel-haired brown ground is favoured for many Hamadan rugs. A distinguishing feature of Hamadan rugs is the fringe which is normally one-sided, with the other having a narrow selvedge.

Description of plate: Hamadan, wool pile, c.1930. 6′ 8″ × 3′ 9″ (2·03 × 1·15 m).

Specification: *Size* – 4′ × 6′ (1·22 × 1·83 m); 2′ 6″ × 8′ 6″ (0·99 × 2·59 m) up to 4′ × 20′ (1·22 × 6·10 m) proportionally. *Loom* – vertical. *Warp* – cotton. *Weft* – cotton, normally single thread, occasionally wool. *Pile* – wool. *Knot* – Turkish, 30 – 100 knots per square inch.

Mazlaghan

Location of manufacture: Mazlaghan rugs are made in Kerdor village, north-east of Hamadan.

General description: They are technically similar to Hamadan and belong to the Hamadan group. A distinctive design – the field is divided by two zig-zag lines within which is a central medallion. The corners have a close design of stars and rosettes, while the borders are standard three-band. Common colours are blue, red and natural camél.

Specification: similar to Hamadan.

Lilihan

Location of manufacture: Lilihan rugs come from the area of Arak, and are woven by Armenians. Technically, however, they belong to the Hamadan group.

General description: Technically similar to Hamadan rugs. The designs are mainly floral executed in beautiful shades of red and blue, amongst others. The motif is stylised and large. It is often repeated in a smaller form as a border.

Specification: similar to Hamadan.

Mushkabad

Location of manufacture: Mushkabad rugs are made mainly in the vicinity of the town of Arak, yet technically belong to the Hamadan group.

General description: Hamadan group. Floral designs are favoured. The rugs and carpets have a deep pile.

Specification: similar to Hamadan.

Description of plate: Hamadan, wool pile, c.1910. 5′ 8″ × 3′ 3″ (1·72 × 0·99 m).

63

Heriz

Location of manufacture: Heriz is a name applied to the rugs of a group of some 30 villages that lie within a radius of 30 miles (48 km) of Tabriz in north-west Iran.

General description: Heriz rugs are the country cousins of the Tabriz, for although they follow many of the designs of the latter they are modified in a way typically their own. The country weavers of Heriz preferred, for example, to weave curvilinear patterns as did the weavers of Tabriz. The curvilinear patterns and scrolls of the arabesque, so much favoured by the weavers of Tabriz, are therefore converted into rectilinear designs of horizontal, diagonal and perpendicular lines. It is this feature which greatly aids their identification. In comparison to the rugs of Tabriz, theirs are simple yet somewhat stylised.

Heriz rugs have been extremely successful in export markets over a considerable period of time, a fact perhaps which has influenced the weavers to stick to their rectilinear designs rather than follow that of their neighbours Tabriz. Some of the older and finer carpets are named after the village of Gorevan. These usually have light backgrounds with beautiful designs in various shades including browns and blues. Other villages in the Heriz group are also occasionally identified with a rug. The more important are Ahar, Bakshis, Mehriban and Jamalbad.

In comparison to the rugs of Tabriz, in the weft of Heriz, the individual knots at the back of the rug give a 'bead-like' appearance. The weft is irregular in thickness.

Specification: *Size* – sizes similar to Tabriz, though not as large. *Loom* – vertical. *Warp* – cotton. *Weft* – cotton. *Pile* – wool. *Knot* – Turkish. *Motif* – Rectilinear interpretations of arabesques and scrolls.

Description of plate: Heriz, runner, wool pile, c.1920. 9′6″ × 3′0″ (2·90 × 0.91 m).

64

Isfahan

Location of manufacture: Situated virtually in the centre of Iran, once the capital city. The rugs are woven in the city itself and in the surrounding villages.

Isfahan carpets and rugs are perhaps the most famous of all oriental floor coverings. They were almost certainly the first to attract the attention of Europe. During the early 17th century, their name was renowned. Although rug making was interrupted by the Afghan invasion, after which her craftsmen switched to textiles and other handicrafts, Isfahan quickly re-established itself as a major centre for quality carpets, after weaving was re-introduced at the turn of the century.

General description: Although many of the antique rugs from Isfahan are of silk, some with gold and silver threads, most of the Isfahan rugs are of wool. The city is still noted for its silk rugs, however, and some are still made today.

Isfahan rugs were and are made in private houses in the less salubrious part of the town, as well as in the neighbouring villages. They are noted for their antique and floral designs, which were developed by an ustad (master) carpet cartoonist during the beginning of the century. Thus from the collector's point of view, he should note that although the design may appear old the rug may not be contemporary with it. Antique Isfahans date from before the Afghan invasions of Persia.

Rugs and carpets with floral motifs generally take the form of a central floral medallion on a field covered with interlaced floral motifs. In some cases the floral design of the central medallion is repeated in the four corners. A typical variation of the

Description of plate: Isfahan, wool pile, c.1930. 7′ 4″ × 4′ 6″ (2·24 × 1·37 m).

use of floral motifs is the innovation of the 'vase and flowers' design. In this, the vase is placed at the bottom of the carpet and the flowers spray outwards in all directions, covering the entire field. This design is occasionally placed within a cartouche, leaving the four corners for additional floral motifs or left plain. A variation of the vase and flowers motif is the double vase and flowers, with vases at each end and flowers meeting in the centre.

The central border band very often has its motif in elaborate herati pattern. The flanking narrow guards, are usually enclosed by thin Greek key pattern bands. Where the central design is floral or faunal, it is not unusual for the design to be adapted in the central border band. The colour range is varied and beautiful, the hall-mark being the ingenuity of their combinations with highlights contrasting with deep shades, which creates such attractive carpets.

Specification: *Size* – variable, most sizes from about 4′ × 6′ (1·22 × 1·83 m) upwards. *Loom* – vertical. *Warp* – cotton. *Weft* – cotton. *Pile* – wool, sometimes silk, closely cut. *Knot* – Persian, high density ranging from about 140 to 400 knots per square inch, while silk rugs have a higher density of about 650 per square inch. *Motifs* – floral, medallions, vase motifs with herati border.

Description of plate: Isfahan, picture rug, 'Joseph and the Coat of Many Colours', wool pile, c.1860. 6′ 1″ × 4′ 3″ (1·85 × 1·30 m).

Kashan

Location of manufacture: Kashans are made in the town of Kashan and its surrounding villages. Situated about 150 miles (241 km) south of Tehran, it is one of the hottest areas of Iran, being just on the edge of the Salt Desert. Water is very scarce.

General description: There have been carpets and rugs made in Kashan at least as far back as the 16th century. Production, however, has not been continuous, for as with the case of Isfahan, it was interrupted by the invasion of Persia in 1722 by the Afghans. Rug making in any quantity was not re-established until the turn of the century, though a few rugs were made from about 1870. Rug making as a small-scale industry was brought about by textile merchants, who turned to the rug trade after their own trade had been hit by imported merchandise.

Kashan quality is noticeable at once. The wool of the early carpets (Kashan Motashemi) is especially good, which imparts to the carpets a smooth velvety quality all their own. It is said that the wool was imported from Australia.

Kashans are highly treasured and classed among the very best Persian carpets and rugs. They are easily recognisable by their distinctive design. The field is covered with floral motifs and they almost invariably have a central medallion. At each end these medallions branch into coronet-like flowering tendrils. In each of the corners is a motif

Description of plate: Kashan, all silk embossed pile, flat weave background in silk with cotton weft, c. 1900. 6′ 7″ × 4′ 4″ (2·00 × 1·32 m).

70

71

resembling the central medallion. Kashans are made without the central medallion but they are not common. Floral decoration, however, is almost invariably the rule and occasionally elaborated with the addition of animal motifs.

The border is always herati and usually surrounded by up to four guards of rosettes etc. Red and dark blue are the common colours, usually in tandem contrasting with each other. The vase and flower 'Hadji Nanoumi' motif is also found.

In a more modern motif, geometric interpretation of classical designs, the entire carpet is knotted in five colours. This kind of rug is known simply as 'Five Colours' or 'panj-rangh'.

A number of pictorial carpets can trace their origin to Kashan. Many of these are in silk pile as well as warp and weft. Silk carpets are not placed on floors in Iran, but are intended as wall decorations.

Specification: *Size* – proportionally 4′ × 7′ (1·22 × 2·13 m), 7′ × 11′ (2·13 × 3·35 m), 11′ × 14′6″ (3·35 × 4·42 m) etc. *Loom* – vertical. *Warp* – cotton. *Weft* – cotton. *Pile* – wool, sometimes silk with silk warp and weft. *Knot* – Persian, 130 – 350 knots to the square inch. Silk – about 600 knots to the square inch.

Description of plate: Kashan, fine wool pile, 19th century. 6′9″ × 4′9″ (2·06 × 1·45 m).

Kerman

Location of manufacture: Isolated from other centres of carpet and rug weaving by hundreds of miles, Kerman is situated in a desolate area in south east Iran. Numerous villages in the surrounding area also produce rugs, all of which are labelled Kerman.

General description: Kerman rugs are extremely beautiful and, in the case of the tightly woven and decorated examples, often recall Persian miniature paintings. Kerman rugs and carpets have been made for some time, but today as part of a major small-scale industry they are made to suit individual export requirements of the British, European and American markets. Subtle differences in preference have been utilised by the ustads, the master carpet designers, and each weaver specialises in a type suited to a particular market. The genius of the ustads of Kerman has always been noticeable in their carpets, as traditional Persian designs have been given the distinctive Kerman touch.

Western influence can be seen in some of the designs, for the rugs from Kerman attracted the attention of overseas importers from an early date and often through patronage subtle changes in designs were introduced.

Kerman carpets are predominately floral, often with a double central medallion. Carpets and rugs often appear to be woven on red grounds which on closer inspection turn out to be self-coloured, the illusion being caused by the density of the red decoration. The motif used on the medallion is also used in the corners and in the border. Pastel shades are popular.

Occasionally animals and more rarely human figures, especially in hunting scenes, can be found on the rugs.

The boteh design, either on its own or as a floral element is fairly common. The 'tree of life' is also found.

Some rugs resemble the lacquer bindings of Persian books, while others resemble the leather bindings of the Koran. In the latter case the design is called ghab Korani.

Two centres near Kerman produce rugs which bear their own name in addition to that of Kerman. They are Kerman Yezd and Kerman Ravar. The latter are extremely fine and good quality rugs. They are made in the village of Ravar, which is about 25 miles (40 km) from Kerman. Rug making at Yezd is a comparatively recent introduction to the town, which is some 150 miles (241 km) to the west of Kerman. Decorative motifs are similar to those of Kerman, but the density of the knotting is lower.

Specification: *Size* – most sizes up to about 11′ 6″ × 16′ 6″ (3·50 × 5·03 m). *Loom* – vertical. *Warp* – cotton. *Weft* – cotton. *Pile* – wool. *Knot* – Persian, basically four qualities – 190, 250, 320 and 400 knots to the square inch.

Description of plate: Kerman, wool pile, 19th century. 7′ 7″ × 4′ 5″ (2·31 × 1·35 m).

Khorasan

Location of manufacture: The province of Khorasan is extremely large, covering a wide area in the north of Iran. The capital is Meshed; the ancient capital was Herat, now part of Afghanistan, Meshed itself is nearly 100 miles (161 km) from the Afghanistan border and only 60 miles (96 km) from the border with Russian Turkestan. The label Khorasan is normally only given to antique rugs from the area. More modern rugs are labelled Meshed. Birjand is another centre but is nearly 240 miles (384 km) south of Meshed; nearby is Mud, another village noted for its rugs. We can divide Khorasan into three groups – Khorasan itself, Meshed and Birjand, with the addition of Mud.

General description: Khorasan carpets are readily recognisable by a peculiarity of the weft. Normally single thread weft is used, but every seven to ten wefts it is increased to three. This causes the back of the carpet to have a banded appearance. The most common decorative motif is the herati in its original form. The herati motif in fact originated in Khorasan, at the ancient capital of Herat from whence it got its name. Herat today (now in Afghanistan) is no longer a rug producing centre.

The herati motif on Khorasan rugs and carpets covers the entire field, with the border too decorated with the herati border motif. The herati motif is not enclosed in a central diamond. The guards utilise boteh motifs or rosettes. The boteh is also used for the border in older carpets. Colours tend to be bright in carpets from the south of the region while in the north they are more subdued.

Specification: *Size* – various, especially large rugs – some up to 20 feet (6·10 m) long. *Loom* – vertical. *Warp* – cotton. *Weft* – cotton. *Pile* – wool. *Knot* – Persian, densely knotted.

Description of plate: Khorasan, wool pile, c.1880. 4′ 9″ × 3′ 4″ (1·45 × 1·02 m).

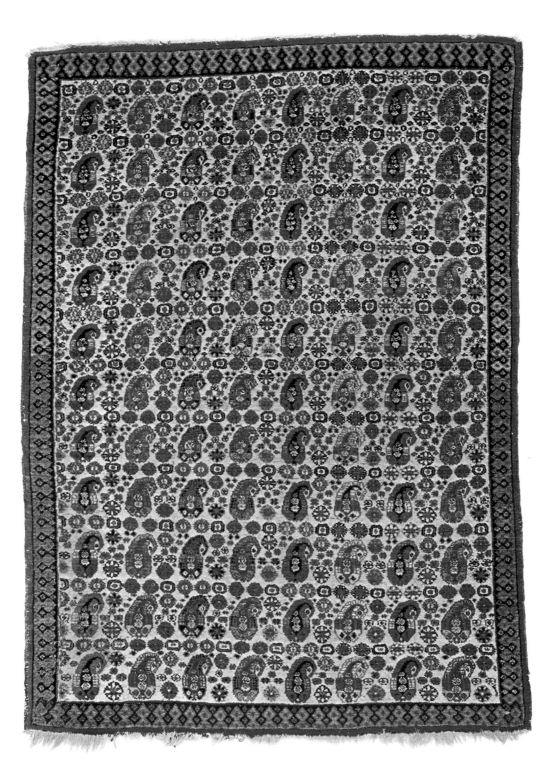

Mahal

see also Feraghan

Location of manufacture: Mahal rugs, like those of Lilihan and Mushkabad come from the town and area of Arak, but like them are generally considered to belong to the Hamadan group.

General description: Similar to Hamadan, they can be distinguished from the main group by virtue of their much larger knot. The pile is notably soft. Designs are geometrical, with a central diamond; floral designs are also common. Borders are similar to Hamadan.

Specification: Technically similar to Hamadan with the exception of their large knot.

Description of plate: Mahal, wool pile, c.1890. 6′ 7″ × 4′ 6″ (2·01 × 1·38 m).

78

Malayer

Location of manufacture: The town of Malayer is situated west of Feraghan.

General description: Malayer carpets are similar to Feraghan and are of very high quality. The designs are tasteful and similar to Feraghan. The colours are mainly blue and red.

Specification: *Size* – various, ranging in proportion up to about $8' \times 20'$ ($2 \cdot 44 \times 6 \cdot 10$ m). *Loom* – vertical. *Warp* – cotton. *Weft* – cotton. *Pile* – wool. *Knot* – Persian, about 80 – 160 knots per square inch. *Motifs* – similar to Feraghan.

Description of plate: Malayer, bag face or sample rug, wool pile, c.1920. $2' 3'' \times 2' 3''$. ($0 \cdot 69 \times 0 \cdot 69$ m).

Meshed

Location of manufacture: Meshed is the modern capital of Khorasan, in north Iran. It is near both the Russian Turkestan and the Afghanistan borders. A great collecting centre for carpets made in the area. A number of nomad rugs come from the town, which is frequented by Uzbek, Turkoman and Huzra tribesmen.

General description: Two kinds of Meshed rugs can be distinguished, those tied with the Persian knot and the Turkbaff of Turkish Meshed, i.e. those tied with the Turkish knot. The latter are produced by Turkish speaking weavers.

Like Khorasan rugs, Mesheds are usually decorated with all-over designs, floral, mainly herati or islim. The latter found on Turkbaff rugs is a meandering floral line that winds its way over the centre field. Turkish Meshed normally have round central medallions. Boteh is also favoured.

Colours are varied, and are bright. Red (especially plum) is favoured, so is a purple-rose. Green is also popular.

The border normally reflects the central motif, while the two narrow flanking guards are also floral.

Specification: *Size* – various, expecially long rugs – some up to 20 feet (6·10 m) long. *Loom* – vertical. *Warp* – cotton. *Weft* – cotton. *Pile* – wool. *Knot* – Persian, densely woven.

Birjand

Location of manufacture: Location is about 240 miles (386 km) south of Meshed.

General description: Similar to that of Meshed. Classical floral designs are favoured, with central medallion. Orange is popular.

Specification: *Size* – various, especially long rugs – some up to 20 feet (6·10 m) long. *Loom* – vertical. *Warp* – cotton. *Weft* – cotton. *Pile* – wool. *Knot* – Persian, densely knotted.

Description of plate: Meshed, wool pile, c.1940. 6′ 7″ × 4′ 3″ (2·00 × 1·29 m).

Mud

Location of manufacture: Mud is a village in Khorasan, in north Iran, about 250 miles (402 km) south of the capital Meshed.

General description: Rugs and carpets from Mud belong to the Khorasan group and are related to both Birjand, which is nearby, and those of Meshed to the north. Although carpets from Mud generally have the same characteristics as those of Birjand, they can normally be distinguished by the fact that they have a thicker pile and by the preference of self-coloured fields.

Specification: *Size* – various, especially long-rugs – some up to 20 feet (6·10 m). *Loom* – vertical. *Warp* – cotton. *Weft* – cotton. *Pile* – wool. *Knot* – Persian, densely knotted.

Description of plate: Mud (Khorasan), wool pile, c.1930. 6′5″ × 4′3″ (1·96 × 1·29 m).

85

Qum

Location of manufacture: Situated between Tehran and Kashan it is about 90 miles (145 km) south of the capital of Iran. Lying as it does in the Iranian highlands, the town of Qum has an ancient and colourful history. It is famous for its golden domed mosque and for the mausoleum of Shah Abbas. The tomb of Fatima is also situated here and is a major centre of pilgrimage for Shiite moslems. It occupies a crossroads position with other important cities.

General description: Contrary to some theories, rug-making is essentially a recent introduction at Qum. The first looms were established in the 1930's at the instigation of a group of Kashan merchants. Qum is, in fact, a great success story in modern rug-weaving, for in spite of its late start, which may have been due to the lack of a ready supply of wool, it has gained for itself a reputation for really high quality rugs. Although a late starter, its rugs are not mere copies of those of other centres, for its designers have adapted and created designs and a style which is distinctly their own. Among the Qum adaptions of other Persian designs may be mentioned the Jozandi Qum i.e. a Qum rug with a Jozan inspired design and boteh motif rugs which are more typically associated with Mir. Isfahan has lent its floral influence, Kashan its love of the central medallion and Bakhtiari has also had its influence too. The zel-i-sultan pattern has also become associated with Qum. In spite of all this, Qum rugs are relatively easy to identify and are not usually confused with the originators of some of these designs. Colours are varied and often vivid, ivory and white being the popular colours for the field. The border is normally composed of three bands; while border herati are found, the central band often takes its motif from the ground design. The border is normally small in relation to the total area of the rug.

The rugs are produced on vertical looms and made as an urban 'cottage' industry, with an average of two looms to each home. The warp is generally of cotton, though occasionally silk is used. Knots which are dense, about 250 – 300 to the square inch are trimmed closely and evenly. The weft is wool, sometimes with the addition of silk.

Specification: *Size* – rugs usually range in proportion – 6' 6" × 9' 9" (1·98 × 2·97 m) to 8' × 11' (2·44 × 3·35 m). *Loom* – vertical. *Warp* – cotton – occasionally silk. *Weft* – wool, sometimes with the addition of silk. *Knot* – Persian, 250 – 300 knots to the square inch, tight and even. *Motifs* – various – including zel-i-sultan; central medallions; floral; boteh etc.

Description of plate: Qum, wool pile, c.1930. 6' 11" × 4' 8" (2·11 × 1·43 m).

86

Sarab

Location of manufacture: Sarab rugs are named after the village where they are made which lies in the north of Iran, near the Caucasian border about 18 miles (29 km) west of Ardebil on the route to Tabriz.

General description: Because of its proximity to the Caucasus many of the rugs made in this village are geometric in character and show marked Caucasian influence. The village is known principally for its runners and stair carpets.

The most common design consists of a camel or natural ground on which a design of geometric shapes within and without diamonds has been knotted. A characteristic of these rugs is the border, which often has a plain outside strip, the same as the main ground. Quality is high and the general appearance attractive. Designs are sometimes similar to Heriz.

Specification: *Size* – runners and strips predominate. *Loom* – vertical. *Warp* – cotton. *Weft* – cotton, sometimes wool. *Pile* – wool. *Knot* – Turkish fairly dense, about 60 – 120 knots per square inch. *Motif* – geometric, Caucasian influence.

Description of plate. *Section and detail*: Sarab, wool pile, runner, 19th century. 13′ 11″ × 3′ 8″ (4·24 × 1·12 m). Typical Caucasian design with unusual additions of human, animal and bird figures (see detail).

Saruq

Location of manufacture: Saruq rugs originated in the village of that name in the region of Arak, although the term can also describe rugs from the town of Arak or the villages in the region.

General description: Old Saruq rugs, produced up to the end of the 19th century, are of very high quality, although this quality has not been maintained in rugs from the Sultanabad weaving complex which bear the name. While some Saruq rugs are produced to traditional designs, many are designed for export and the American market in particular.

The early examples made before the First World War have a tendency to tear, due to the weft having been pushed down hard against the knots. Traditional decoration consists of a central medallion and although the designs are fundamentally floral, they are angular in execution. The boteh motif is often used, particularly in older rugs. The border usually consists of two grounds, decorated with rosettes and wavy lines, surrounding a wider central band often decorated with border herati. Modern Saruqs are characterised by a blue weft, whereas old examples have a weft of undyed or very pale blue cotton.

Traditional colours include a ground of orange-red, toned down with ivory, dark blue and green and the frequent use of turquoise in the decoration, while on rugs intended for the Western market, pink is common.

Specification: *Size* – all the common Persian shapes as well as runners. *Loom* – vertical. *Warp* – cotton. *Weft* – cotton. *Pile* – wool. *Knot* – Persian, 160 to 400 knots per square inch.

Description of plates. *Top*: Saruq, wool pile, c.1910. 7′ 1″ × 4′ 6″ (2·16 × 1·37 m). *Bottom*: Saruq, wool pile, c.1880. 7′ 0″ × 4′ 7″ (2·14 × 1·40 m).

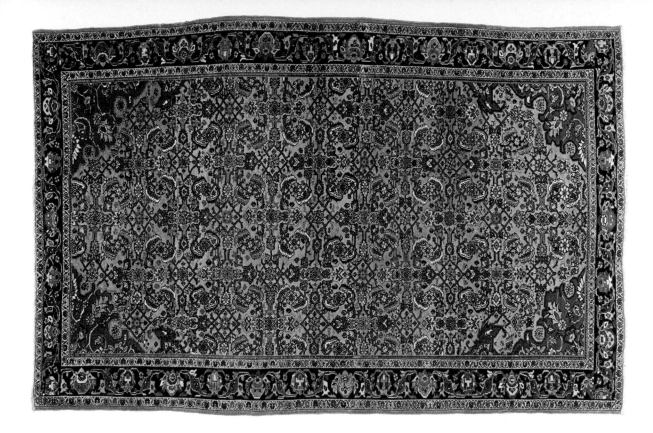

Senneh

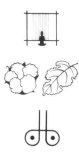

Location of manufacture: The small town of Senneh is the capital of Persian 'Kurdistan'. Situated south of the town of Bijar and north-west of Hamadan, it is situated in a fertile valley.

General description: The fine rugs and kelims of Senneh have been famous for over two hundred years. A strange fact is that it has given its name to the traditional Persian knot, although the Senneh weavers almost exclusively use the Turkish or Ghiordes knot. While most rugs can be identified by their designs, Senneh rugs can be identified easily by the blind, because they have a particular granular feel which is unique to rugs made in the town. It is quite distinctive and can easily be separated from other Kurdistan weaves including that of Bijar. This feel is achieved by using fine twisted yarn for the knots. The warp, which can be cotton or silk, is almost invisible and the weft lines often irregular and wavy. The knots are very close and tight, often numbering 500 to the square inch. The pile is short and thick.

The colouring of Senneh rugs is always harmonious and attractive with red, blue and green predominating in the darker colours and yellow and white in the lighter range. Designs are varied, with a preference for herati and boteh motifs. In the former, the herati can cover the whole rug including the border. The use of the boteh motif can be most imaginative when not used in the conventional vertical lines. Sometimes the boteh is employed in a circular design forming a rose, each boteh acting as a petal. Each circular motif thus formed would combine with others to cover the whole rug. When employed in a regular vertical pattern the boteh is usually larger than normal. The flower of Mirza Ali motif (gul-i-Mirza Ali) is also found. It is normally combined with a herati border.

The normal Senneh border consists of three bands, the centre one being an accentuated angular form of the border herati. Border boteh are also found.

Specification: *Size* – standard. *Loom* – vertical. *Warp* – cotton or silk. *Weft* – cotton or silk. *Pile* – wool. *Knot* – Turkish – up to 500 knots per square inch. *Motifs* – herati – all over or in medallion, indicated by contrasting ground colour, boteh, gul-i-Mirza Ali etc.

Description of plate: Senneh, fine wool pile, c.1870. 6′ 4″ × 4′ 5″ (1·94 × 1·35 m).

Shiraz

Location of manufacture: The city of Shiraz is situated in the south of Iran and is the capital of the Fars province. Today no carpets or rugs are made in the town, although considering that Shiraz is in the centre of a rug making area for which it is the market town, it is unlikely that rugs were not made there at some time. The term Shiraz, however, is now taken to indicate rugs made by nomadic tribes which inhabit the Fars province and which are marketed at the bazaar in Shiraz. These tribes include the Qashqa'i, Ainalu, Baharlu, Keshkuli and Farsimadan.

General description: Shiraz rugs are normally found proportionally in the following sizes – 6′ 6″ × 9′ 10″ (1·98 × 3·00 m), 8′ × 11′ (2·44 × 3·35 m), 4′ 6″ × 6′ 6″ (1·37 × 1·98 m), 6′ 3″ × 8′ 3″ (1·91 × 2·52 m). The decoration is nomad in spirit executed in bright colours. The designs are simple, geometric and bold. A characteristic design, a trade mark of Shiraz, is the diamond lozenge employed either on its own or in a series of two or three down the centre of the rug. The diamond is almost invariably in blue, either dark or light, on a red ground closely decorated with stylised plant motifs, a theme which is also taken up by the border. The border itself usually consists of a wide central band flanked by narrow bands. At each end there can be a band of diagonal stripes.

Specification: *Sizes* – 6′ 6″ × 9′ 10″ (1·98 × 3·00 m) to 8′ × 11′ (2·44 × 3·35 m), 4′ 6″ × 6′ 6″ (1·37 × 1·98 m) to 6′ 3″ × 8′ 3″ (1·91 × 2·52 m). *Loom* – horizontal. *Warp* – wool. *Weft* – wool (single or double). Cotton is occasionally used by the semi-nomadic tribes. *Pile* – wool. *Knot* – both Persian and Turkish knots are used, fairly loose, maximum about 100 knots to the square inch. *Motifs* – nomad. *Quality* – variable. Colours, red, blue, ground sometimes cream.

Description of plate: Shiraz, wool pile, c.1920. 7′ 2″ × 5′ 10″ (2·18 × 1·78 m).

Shiraz-Kelim

 Location of manufacture: Shiraz, the capital city of Fars province is situated in the south of Iran. It is a marketing centre for rugs made by nomadic tribes of the area.

General description: A kelim (the word comes from the Turkish meaning 'prayer rug') is a tapestry woven rug as opposed to a knotted rug with pile. The design is, in fact, formed by the thick weft which faces the rug and which hides the warp. They are not as sturdy as knotted rugs and hence really old examples are rare – as the warp generally breaks down, causing the rug to disintegrate. (See page 33). Kelims in the East are generally not used for floor coverings but instead are used as bed, sofa and divan coverings, or even door or window hangings.

Shiraz kelims follow typical nomad designs with the large diamond, either single or up to three in a row, predominating. Many are believed to have been made by the Qashqa'i tribe.

Specification: *Size* – proportionally from about 6′ × 9′ (1·83 × 2·74 m) to 8′ × 11′ (2·44 × 3·35 m). *Loom* – kelim. *Warp* – cotton. *Weft* – wool, cotton. *Knots* – none, kelim weave. *Pile* – none, weft face. *Motifs* – nomad.

Description of plate: Shiraz kelim – wool flat woven, c.1890. 9′ × 5′ 4″ (2·74 × 1·63 m).

97

Shiraz-Niriz

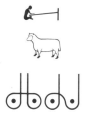

Location of manufacture: Niriz is some 99 miles (160 km) south east of Shiraz.

General description: 19th and early 20th century rugs classified as Niriz were probably made by weavers of the Baharlu or Nafar tribes, the two major tribes of the area. Rugs bearing this name are often confused with the work of Afshar or Qashqa'i, and have been classified as such. Close examination will, however, separate them from both these attributions, especially Afshar. Here we classify them as peripheral Shiraz type. The rugs are nomad in type and technically similar to the specifications for Shiraz – they can be distinguished by the fact that they have overtones of Qashqa'i and Afshar, while dominated by Shiraz ideas. The weft is almost concealed.

Specification: *Sizes* – 6′ × 9′ (1·83 × 2·74 m) to 8′ × 11′ (2·44 × 3·35 m), 4′ 6″ × 6′ 6″ (1·37 × 1·98 m) to 6′ 3″ × 8′ 3″ (191 × 2·52 m). *Loom* – horizontal. *Warp* – wool. *Weft* – wool, cotton occasionally used. *Pile* – wool. *Knot* – both Persian and Turkish, fairly loose, maximum about 100 knots to the square inch, though often a lot less. *Motif* – nomad, quality variable. Colours, red and blue grounds, sometimes cream. Alternating colours are a feature.

Description of plate: Shiraz-Niriz, wool pile, c.1870. 8′ 4″ × 5′ 6″ (2·54 × 1·68 m).

Tabriz

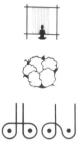

Location of manufacture: Tabriz has had a chequered history – it has been invaded by armies and devastated by earthquakes several times. Situated as it is in the north-west of Iran, it was at one time the capital of Iran, although its people are Turkish in both origin and language. Since the mid 19th century, it has been a major centre for the manufacture of rugs and carpets.

General description: Rugs and carpets have been made at Tabriz for centuries, but it has only been a major producer since the mid 19th century, when merchants found that export demand necessitated putting the industry on a 'factory' basis. Today few rugs or carpets are produced in private houses, the majority of the production being centred in small factories. The looms are vertical, often with metal rollers, and some are massive, producing carpets up to 30/35 feet (10m) wide. Since the mid 19th century, designs have been made specifically to meet the export market and are therefore geared in some ways to satisfying European taste. Thus rugs from Tabriz can be found in most colours. The late 19th century industry owes much to three master weavers, especially to Haji Jalil who was famed for his silk carpets. Around the fifties (20th century) another weaver became popular – one Taba Tabaie. Although not of course antiques, his carpets may be equally sought after by the end of this century.

Rugs and carpets were and are made in all sizes. Both Persian and Turkish knots are found, though the symmetrical Turkish predominates. Several qualities are known, with densities ranging from about 64 to 400 knots to the square inch. Thus there is a great variation in appearance between high and low quality rugs. In fine rugs, the pile is extremely compact but can be somewhat coarse, as the wool itself is coarse, a feature which is often accentuated by the fact that it is dyed and washed in water with a high salt content. Some of the finest carpets, made especially at the turn of the century, had silk piles. The warp and weft are both cotton, with the weft being double.

There is a great variety of designs, with many antique and traditional motifs being borrowed from other areas. They have also created their own designs which are unlike those of other Persian rugs. Rugs with large central medallions surrounded by floral motifs are common. Hunting patterns are also found. Borders are always exquisite; composed with three guards, the main band normally repeats the ground motif. Herati designs are found but are somewhat rare.

Specification: *Size* – most sizes up to the very large. *Loom* – vertical. *Warp* – cotton. *Weft* – cotton, of variable thickness. *Pile* – wool, silk. Wool pile can be uneven and rough. *Knot* – Turkish, sometimes Persian, between 64 to 400 knots to the square inch. *Motifs* – varied with preference to central medallions and floral motifs. *Colours* – varied.

Description of plate: Tabriz, wool pile, c.1880. 5′ 10″ × 4′ 5″ (1·78 × 1·35 m).

Kurdistan

Location of manufacture: Kurdish carpets generally come from Kurdish tribes living in western Iran on the border with Iraq.

General description: Kurdish carpets are on the whole coarse in comparison to the sophisticated rugs of Senneh, the capital of Kurdistan. The rugs and carpets of Senneh are quite different. Kurdish rugs have deep piles which are irregularly cut. The designs are primitive. The warp and weft are of wool, as is the pile.

Specification: *Size* – various, generally not large. *Loom* – horizontal. *Warp* – wool. *Weft* – wool. *Pile* – wool. *Knot* – Turkish, 60 – 80 knots per square inch.

Description of plate: Kurdistan, wool pile, c.1860. 6′ 8″ × 4′ 2″ (2·03 × 1·27 m).

Description of plate: Kurdish, bag face, wool pile, c.1920. 3′ 8″ × 2′ 7″ (1·12 × 0·79 m).

Luristan

Location of manufacture: The name of Luristan is synonymous with one of the most ancient civilizations of Persia. A mountainous area, it lies in the south-west of Iran.

General description: The rugs are woven on a horizontal loom by members of the nomadic Luri tribe. Decorative motifs are geometric and unsophisticated. A common motif consists of three large diamonds linked together point to point, which extend along the length of the rug. A Greek key design sometimes follows the outline of the diamond, while the diamond area itself occasionally has a linear or geometric motif. The alternative design is the stepped diamond. Stylised and linear 'trees of life', either alone or several, are also popular motifs.

The borders reflect the design of the field, and consist of three bands, one slightly larger than the others, plus occasionally additional guards.

Colours tend to be drab yet bright with an almost luminous quality, created by yellows, whites and light blues standing out of a background of red or blue.

In spite of their rather deep pile of coarse wool, they are of good quality.

Specification: *Size* – large carpets are not found, the normal size is about 5′ × 8′ (1·53 × 2·45 m), though smaller rugs are found.

Description of plate: Luristan, bag face, wool pile. c.1900. 3′ 8″ × 2′ 9″ (1·12 × 0·84 m).

Qashqa'i

Location of manufacture: The Qashqa'i are a large confederation of tribes, nomadic or seasonally migrant, whose territory extends over a large area of the Fars highlands north-west of Shiraz.

General description: They are in many respects similar to the rugs and carpets of Shiraz but are of a much higher quality. The designs have a number of similarities to the Caucasian, a fact which the Qashqa'i themselves attribute to their having settled in Azerbaijan on the journey south from their ancestral homelands in Central Asia. The Qashqa'i today consist of a confederacy of tribes, mainly Turkish in origin, but with some Arab, Fars and Kurd blood. Their name is thought to have come from 'Qashqa' – the Turkish word for 'horse with white blaze' – a sign which was considered lucky.

The rugs of the Qashqa'i have traditionally been woven by women, as have many of the rugs of other nomadic tribes. The first rugs were made by the Keshkuli and Shesh Baluki tribes. Qashqa'i rugs can easily be distinguished from those of Shiraz and of the 'copies' made by the neighbouring Khamseh confederation, by their designs and weave.

The weave is fine and relatively neat; the weft is distinctive, being normally coloured a shade of red. Designs often consist of a diamond shaped centre with the ground covered with small geometrically stylised figures of birds, dogs and other animals, with the addition of rosettes, stars, crosses and petals. The normal colours are reddish-brown, red, cream and blue. The warp and weft is wool, sometimes mixed with cattle hair, while the pile is high quality wool. Knots are predominantly Persian, though Turkish knots are sometimes found.

Specification: *Size* – similar to Shiraz. *Loom* – horizontal. *Warp* – wool. *Weft* – wool. *Pile* – wool. *Knot* – Persian and Turkish. *Motifs* – Nomad, preference of diamond-shaped central lozenge with geometric animals and flowers.

Description of plates. *Top*: Qashqa'i, wool pile, mid 19th century. 6′2″ × 4′4″ (1·88 × 1·32 m). *Bottom*: Qashqa'i, bag, wool pile. c.1890. 1′9″ × 1′8″ (0·53 × 0·51 m).

Anatolian

Location of manufacture: Anatolia – 'Land of the Rising Sun' – is the name given to the Asian part of Turkey, in particular that part which extends from the Taurus mountain range in the south-east of Turkey to the central plateau.

General description: The name Anatolian is often given to a rug which is Turkish by manufacture but to which no closer attribution can be made. In a way it is a label of convenience. It can, however, be more specific and generally be taken to indicate rugs made by two principal groups – Mudjur and Kirshehir and woven in villages of the same name; and Yuruk and Yahyali which are produced by nomadic tribes. Generally however, the term Anatolian can refer to rugs made over a wide area and include rugs woven both by village craftsmen and nomads.

Because of the variation in the place of manufacture there is also a variation in looms used and of course in quality and inspiration. Wool is normally chosen for the pile and for the weft and warp, though in the latter cotton is occasionally found. The knot is always Turkish, varying in density between 40 and 100 per square inch.

Yuruk rugs are mainly geometric in design. A popular design was a hexagonal motif surrounded by a key design known as the 'running dog' motif. The area within the hexagon would be decorated with a design of diamonds of various sizes, within each other, each of a varying colour. Outside the hexagon at each corner would be an octagon within which would be an eight-pointed star. Borders are wide and usually composed of four guards containing geometric leaf motifs. Colours are vivid but pleasingly combined. They include violet, yellow, green, blue and orange.

The rugs of Yahyali are similar to Yuruk but are simpler in design. The number of diamonds and/or hexagons are reduced, and gone is the running dog key. The overall effect is much closer to the Caucasian. Shapes are more elongated and colours darker, more sedate.

Specification: *Size* – between 3′ 3″ – 6′ 6″ (0·99 × 1·98m) proportionally or 3′ 3″ × 11′ 6″ (0·99 × 3·50 m) proportionally. *Loom* – Yuruk and Yahyali – horizontal. Mudjur and Kirshehir vertical. *Warp* – wool. *Weft* – wool. *Pile* – wool. *Knot* – Turkish, 40 to 100 knots per square inch. *Motifs* – geometric including hexagons, diamonds, running dog, stars etc. Also prayer rugs.

Description of plate: Anatolian prayer rug, wool pile, c.1900. 5′ 7″ × 3′ 9″ (1·70 × 1·15 m).

Bergama

Location of manufacture: The town of Bergama, a town about 30 miles (48 km) to the north of Izmir, on the Mediterranean coast in west Turkey, was originally known as Pergamon. Its name was changed earlier this century by Ataturk. Rugs bearing this name do not, however, originate in the town but from villages in the large area to the north and east of the town. The rugs were and are made principally by weavers of nomadic or semi-nomadic origin. Small factories are also thought to have existed in or near the town from an early date but Bergama was mainly a market centre. Carpets and rugs thought to be from this area are shown in early paintings, in particular 'The Ambassadors' by Hans Holbein in 1533, now in the National Gallery in London.

General description: The villages of the Bergama group produced rugs decorated with a large variety of designs and motifs, which often appear to have no common denominator. Close examination will, however, reveal traits which suggest a common origin. A feature which the Bergama weavers seemed to have favoured was the square or nearly square rug. The centre of the rugs usually have a large rectangle which dominates the rug. Another distinctive feature is the use of the eight-pointed star, which may be set within an octagon, square or circle. The flavour is distinctly primitive, of geometric character with Caucasian overtones. In fact in the latter respect they are sometimes confused with the rugs of Kazak. Distinctive colours for the motifs are white, orange, and azure. Squares and octagons are often outlined in blue or other colours.

Specification: *Size* – in proportion from about 2′ 6″ × 3′ 6″ (0·76 × 1·06 m) to 5′ × 6′ 3″ (1·52 × 1·98 m) or even squares. *Loom* – horizontal. *Warp* – wool (late examples cotton). *Weft* – wool, (late examples – cotton). *Pile* – wool, good quality, and deep. Lustrous red, normally two or three rows, which form a strip easily seen in the back of the rug. *Knot* – Turkish, low density, between 30 and 80 knots per square inch. *Motifs* – geometric, particularly eight-pointed star, rectangles, octagons etc.

Description of plate: Bergama, prayer rug, wool pile, c.1800. 3′ 10″ × 3′ 7″ (1·17 × 1·09 m).

Ghiordes

Location of manufacture: The town of Ghiordes, which has given its name to the Turkish knot, is situated in western Turkey about 60 miles (97 km) from Izmir, the port on the Mediterranean coast.

General description: The antique rugs of Ghiordes are amongst the finest in all Turkey. Indeed at one time they were so highly thought of that they were being faked at Panderma. Today, however, rugs from the town are of poor quality, a faded echo of a once great art. Ghiordes rugs can be divided into two groups – those dating from the 16th to early 19th century, and those dating from the 19th century onwards, (modern rugs excluded). They can be easily distinguished apart from design, quality and other features, by their colours. Rugs in the first group tend to have dull and sedate colours, while those in the second are much more lively.

With the occasional exception proving the rule, Ghiordes rugs are exclusively prayer rugs. The finer examples are richly decorated. There are a number of features distinctive of Ghiordes. The janina design is one. This design resembles two exotic and brightly coloured fruits set between a vertical leaf to which they are joined. This stylised flower/fruit motif is found on the borders of some of the rugs dating to the 19th century, as well as some modern ones. The prayer niche or mihrab which is outlined by a thin notched border, is usually placed between two wide but shallow rectangular areas, one above and one below the niche. The ground is decorated with highly stylised flowers and fruit. The mihrab may be supported by two columns, one on each side, while from the central pinnacle may emerge a floral motif that appears like a hanging lamp.

The niche in the first group is normally coloured ivory, dark blue or occasionally green. Colours used in motifs and borders are somewhat limited. In the second group, the niche is more often red with the motifs and borders in vivid colours, which may include orange, ivory, yellow, red, all merged in perfect harmony.

The rugs were made on small vertical looms. The pile is normally of high quality wool, closely cut. The warp and weft are of cotton; sometimes undyed cotton is also used for knotting special white motifs. Normally two weft threads are spaced between knots. Knots are Turkish, varying in density between 65 and 130 to the square inch. Silk rugs are also known, either silk on cotton warp and weft or all-over silk. Silk rugs normally have a density of about 130 knots to the square inch.

Specification: *Size* – various including all normal prayer rug sizes. *Loom* – vertical. *Warp* – double cotton. *Weft* – cotton. *Pile* – wool (occasionally silk). *Knot* – Turkish, density between 65 and 130 knots per square inch. *Motifs* – Prayer rugs, rectangles above mihrab, janina fruit and flower motif, 'hanging flowers' in mihrab.

Description of plate: Ghiordes, prayer rug, wool pile, c.1800. 6′ 5″ × 4′ 7″ (1·96 × 1·40 m).

Koum Ka Pour

Location of manufacture: The Koum Ka Pour 'factory' was situated in the suburbs of Istanbul. It was in operation for just a short time between 1890 and 1910.

General description: The name Koum Ka Pour ('Gate to the Sands') is associated with some of the finest silk carpets. The factory drew its supply of silk from the filatures of Broussa, as did the factories of Hereke. Rugs at Koum Ka Pour were made under the direction of a master weaver called Kanata, who worked under the patronage of the Sultan. He is said by some to have produced some of the finest rugs in the world. Perhaps because of this far more rugs are attributed to the factory than could have possibly been made during the short time of its existence.

Kanata is said to have been one of the few weavers who was able to work metallic threads of gold and silver into beautiful rose patterns of many colours. The designs were principally drawn from the traditional patterns of Persia, though the knots were Turkish. Both weft and warp were of silk as, of course, was the pile. Colours were pastel and harmonious, set-off by metallic gold and silver.

Specification: *Size* – various. *Loom* – vertical. *Warp* – silk. *Weft* – silk. *Pile* – silk. *Knot* – Turkish extremely fine and dense, up to 1,000 knots per square inch. *Motifs* – mainly antique Persian. Pastel shades with gold and silver thread.

Description of plate: Koum Ka Pour, prayer rug, all silk with gold and silver thread, c.1900. 5′ 4″ × 4′ 2″ (1·63 × 1·27 m).

Makri

Location of manufacture: The town of Makri, present day Fethiye, is situated on the Mediterranean coast near the Island of Rhodes.

General description: The town, which stands on the site of the ancient city of Temessus, changed its name to Fethiye in 1923. Rugs from Makri are often labelled Rhodean as they were originally believed to have been made on the Island and other surrounding offshore islands. Another name applied is the modern name of the town, thus rugs from the town can be called by all the names. It is usual, however, for rugs made prior to 1923 to be called Makri.

Rugs from the town are occasionally grouped with those from Milas, but they are in fact a separate group. A distinctive feature of Makri prayer rugs is the double mihrab, placed side by side divided by a thin column. Colours are generally blue ground, with yellow, natural and orange, and red.

Specification: *Size* – usual sizes for Turkish prayer rugs, others similar to Milas. *Loom* – vertical. *Warp* – wool. *Weft* – wool. *Pile* – wool, slightly coarse. *Knot* – Turkish. *Motif* – distinctive feature of prayer rugs – double mihrab.

Description of plate: Makri, wool pile, mid 19th century. 3′ 8″ × 2′ 2″ (1·12 × 0·66 m).

Milas

Location of manufacture: The town is situated on the shores of the Aegean Sea in the south-west of Turkey.

General description: Like other centres of rug-making in Turkey, Milas made both prayer rugs and conventional rugs. The latter are not easily identified but on close examination have characteristic features which act as useful clues. The first is that the colours are quite bright and include yellow, white, violet, red and a bright blue. The second clue is that the designs, though common to rugs of other Turkish centres have been highly stylised. Examination of the back of the rug will often help, for it may show a fairly regular pattern of lines and knots, with the weft doubled after every two rows of knots.

Prayer rugs are much easier to recognise for the mihrab or niche is fairly distinctive. It is small in relation to the total area of carpet and the top has two triangular indentations, one on each side, which gives it an almost diamond-shaped head. In the centre of the mihrab is sometimes a diamond shape, from which branch either eight-pointed stars in octagons or stylised flower shapes. The diamond may be connected to the base of the mihrab by what appears to be a stem of a plant, with small leaves branching off either side. The border too can be quite distinctive. The wide central band which may consist of serrated diamond motifs separated by stylised flowers, will be flanked on the outside by diagonal bands of differing colours, which in turn are flanked by a wider band of pale colour decorated with rosettes or similar motifs. The inner-most band surrounding the mihrab may also be of diagonal bands. The main colours used for borders tend to be yellow, white, brown, green, and a red (the same as that used for the mihrab). White is normally the ground colour with the mihrab being red, or a dull red-orange.

Specification: *Size* – varying proportionally from about 3′ 6″ × 5′ (1·06 × 1·52 m) and about 5′ 3″ × 8′ 3″ (1·60 × 2·52 m). *Loom* – vertical. *Warp* – wool. *Weft* – wool, double between rows (occasionally both warp and weft are of cotton). *Pile* – wool, medium length. *Knot* – Turkish, density between 60 and 120 knots per square inch.

Description of plate: Milas, prayer rug, wool pile, c.1860. 5′ 7″ × 3′ 3″ (1·70 × 1·00 m).

119

Mudjur

Location of manufacture: Mudjur is situated on the central plateau of Turkey, near the town of Kirshehir. The rugs of both towns are similar.

General description: Mudjur is noted for its prayer rugs as is the nearby town of Kirshehir. The borders of the rugs are usually very wide, reducing the mihrab niche to a small central section of the rug. The border bands are composed of a variety of geometric motifs including the rhombus, star, key and other forms. The niche is invariably self coloured in red, red-brown or green. Other colours are similar to Yuruk, i.e. lilac, green, orange etc. but are more subdued. The rugs of Kirshehir, while similar, are generally paler in colour.

Specification: *Size* – normal prayer rug proportions. *Loom* – vertical. *Warp* – wool. *Weft* – wool. *Pile* – wool. *Knot* – Turkish, between 40 – 100 knots to the square inch. *Motif* – prayer rugs with extremely wide borders composed of a number of bands. *Colours* – red, green, red-brown, lilac, orange, (in Kirshehir – orange becomes yellow, and all colours lighter).

Description of plate: Mudjur prayer rug, wool pile, c.1860. 5′ 5″ × 3′ 4″ (1·65 × 1·02 m).

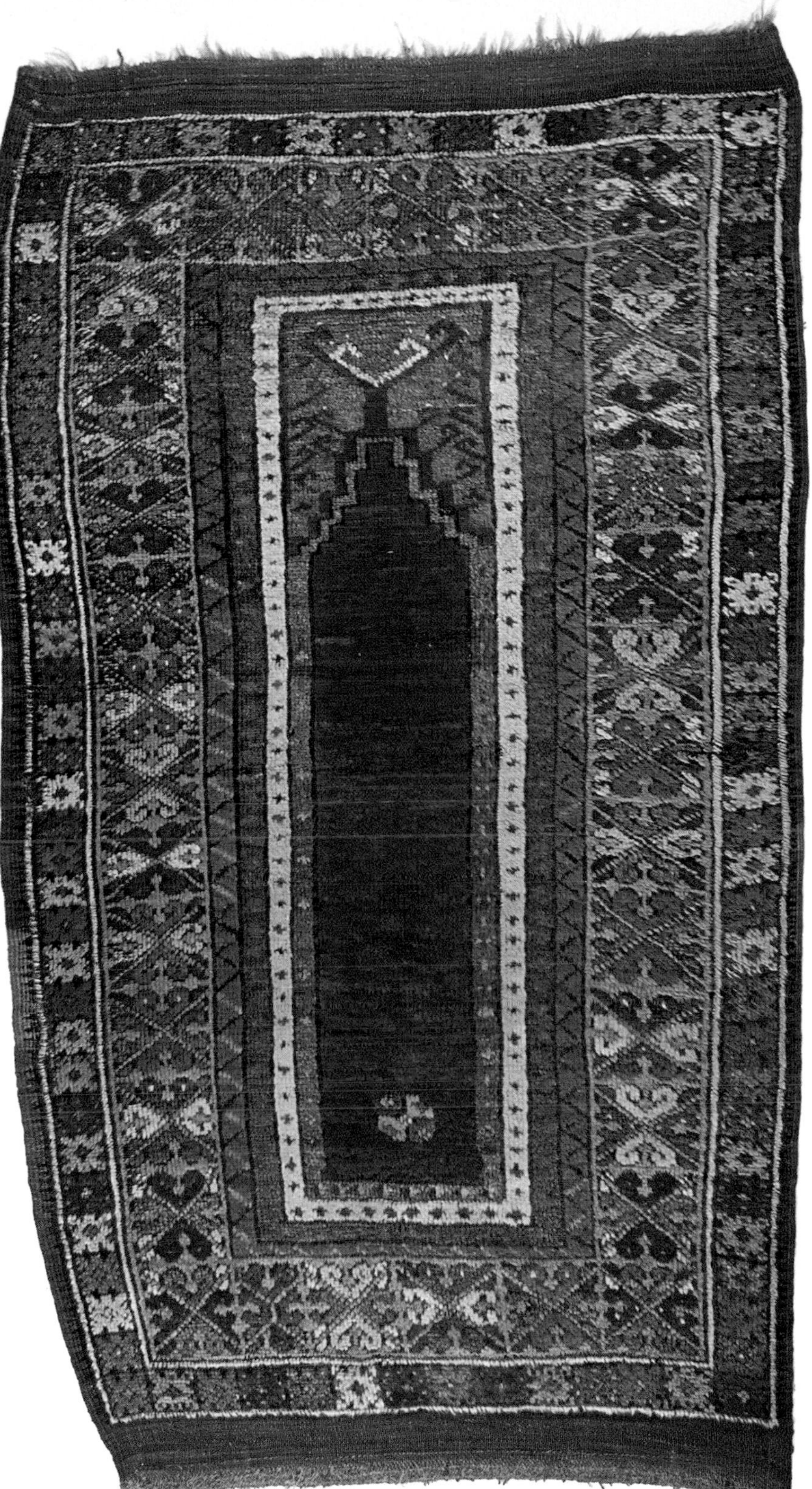

Panderma

Location of manufacture: The town is situated in northern Turkey, near Istanbul.

General description: Rugs have been made at Panderma since at least the late 18th century. Generally speaking, the rugs are not distinctive in design, for the weavers copied many designs from other centres, including some Persian designs. Their aged copies of antique 'Ghiordes' and 'Kula' are perhaps the best known. Close examination will always separate the copies from the rugs of both these centres. One indication is the obvious difference between the weaves, sometimes the only method of detecting wrong attributions. From the back a ripple may be seen similar to that on Caucasian rugs. The knots have a distinctive raised parallel line effect.

   High quality silk rugs from the town of Kayseri are sometimes wrongly labelled Panderma. Both wool and silk rugs were made in the town. Although finely knotted, they tend not to wear as well as other Turkish rugs. A distinguishing feature is the border which tends to be composed of a large number of bands of equal width.

Specification: *Size* – variable. *Loom* – vertical. *Warp* – cotton. *Weft* – cotton. *Pile* – wool (sometimes silk). *Knot* – Turkish, between 60 and 120 knots per square inch. *Motif* – varied, copies of Ghiordes and Kula.

Description of plate: Panderma, prayer rug, wool pile, c.1890. 5′ 10″ × 4′ 7″ (1·78 × 1·40 m).

123

The horizontal loom is primitive but portable, and thus is used by nomadic tribes as well as in some small villages. The following rugs are made on the horizontal loom:– Afshar, Bakhtiari, Shiraz, Niriz, Kurdistan, Luristan, Qashqa'i, Bergama, Chi Chi, Daghestan, Karabagh, Kazak, Kuba, Sejur, Baluchi, Beshir, Salor, Tekke, Yomud, Tibetan, Yuruk, Yahyali.

Description of plate: A nomad weaving a modern rug in traditional colours and materials, on a simple tribal horizontal loom.

Chi Chi

Location of manufacture: Name given to rugs by the Chenchen tribe, in the south of the Caucasus, now part of the Chenchen-Ingush Autonomous Soviet Socialist Republic.

General description: Chi Chi rugs have a very distinctive type of design and colouring. It is unlikely that they were the exclusive preserve of the tribe, however, and Chi Chi rugs are found with a number of different weave patterns of the eastern Caucasian group.

The rugs are made on a horizontal loom and are generally small. Unlike other Caucasian rugs the border may be the dominant feature. The main border displays a feature peculiar to Chi Chi rugs, a pattern composed of slanting oblongs, separating eight-pointed stars or rosettes. This pattern may be repeated in a sub-band, but more often than not other Caucasian features will be found including diamonds, triangles, eight-pointed stars etc. The field is also decorated with these devices, larger of course, and in varying combinations. The norm is lines of alternating octagons and diamonds. The diamonds in this case are often surrounded by an outline of hooked key patterns. The octagons are not usually so treated. Within both diamonds the octagons are stylised floral motifs or eight-pointed stars. Once seen a Chi Chi rug is rarely forgotten. The colours are pleasing and well balanced with yellow, dark blue, brown and red. The background of the main border is normally blue, as is the field.

Specification: *Size* – between 2′ 6″ × 5′ (0·76 × 1·52 m) and 3′ 3″ × 5′ 6″ (0·91 × 1·67 m). *Loom* – horizontal. *Warp* – wool. *Weft* – wool or cotton. *Pile* – short, good quality wool. *Knot* – Turkish, density between 130 and 240 knots per square inch. *Motif* – distinctive border as described above.

Description of plate: Chi Chi (Shirvan), wool pile, c.1900. 5′ × 3′ 9″ (1·52 × 1·14 m).

127

Daghestan

Location of manufacture: A Soviet Socialist Republic in the north-eastern Caucasus, the country spans a large area up to the Caspian Sea.

General description: Identification of Caucasian rugs up to the point of attributing them to centres like Daghestan, Kuba, Derbend, Shirvan etc. can be most difficult – if one recognises that it is probable that designs were freely copied. Weaving features do not offer much help, as they have not been able to be tied to designs in any regular manner. In spite of this difficulty, rugs are still attributed to these Caucasian centres and for the purposes of dealing with Caucasian rugs it may, therefore, be necessary to review the majority of peculiarities of design, colour and weaving, which on average are attributed to these centres.

The rugs we call Daghestan are generally quite old, antique and rare. More modern rugs from the area are known as Derbend. The feature usually associated with Daghestan is the diagonally banded field. In this design the field is divided by narrow diagonal bands of alternating colours, generally in different shades of blue, with white, yellow and pale green. The bands themselves are decorated with hooked squares (i.e. a square from which one opposing corner of each side is a hook), eight-pointed stars and stylised roses, which are interspaced at random.

Another design common to the rugs of Daghestan is the three medallion pattern. In this, the entire centre of the rug is taken up by three large medallions, each of which is composed of three internal geometric shapes, consisting of two outer star shapes, within which is a central square, which is itself decorated with patterns of Caucasian inspiration. Of the stars only the outer one is clearly defined.

Border patterns almost invariably match the central design. They are typically Caucasian and include among other motifs the eight-pointed star. The hooked square pattern is also found as a border.

Specification: *Size* – usually between 2′ 2″ × 5′ (0·66 × 1·52 m) and 3′ 5″ × 10′ (1·04 × 3·05 m). *Loom* – horizontal. *Warp* – wool (brown in colour and thick). *Weft* – wool. *Pile* – deep, good quality wool. *Knot* – Turkish, ranging from 50 – 100 knots per square inch. *Motifs* – diagonal border with hooked squares. N.B. The thick brown warp usually can be clearly seen on the back of the rug. The weft sometimes has a ripple appearance.

Description of plate: Daghestan runner, wool pile, c.1890. 7′ 9″ × 3′ (2·36 × 0·92 m).

Karabagh

Location of manufacture: Karabagh rugs come from a region of that name, in the S.E. Caucasus, which borders N.E. Iran. The people of this area are principally Armenian.

General description: Although rugs from Karabagh lack distinctive designs, they do have a distinctive weave – a feature which will readily separate them from the neighbouring Kazak rugs. If closely examined on the reverse, Karabagh rugs will reveal a double weft between every two rows of knots. It is one of the few distinctive weaves of the Caucasus. In other ways Karabagh rugs are less distinctive, using both Western and Persian inspired patterns, and as a result of this many have been simply labelled Caucasian or Armenian. Two designs traditionally associated with Kazak rugs are now thought to have been made in Karabagh; they are Chelaberd, the so-called 'Eagle Kazak', with its large multi-faceted and structured sunburst medallions which fill the ground of the rug and the Chondzoresk. In the case of the latter it seems probable that they were made at both Karabagh and Kazak.

Common designs include the medallion, boteh and herati patterns as well as Savonnerie inspired designs. The medallion motif is mainly used on stair carpets. In appearance they are similar to those of Khorasan or Feraghan. Thus, the medallions may be almost floral or, on the other hand, geometrical almost diamond shaped. The ground is normally dark in colour with lighter and brightly coloured patterns. The boteh pattern is used in a stylised manner, with the boteh arranged in diagonal lines with the points alternately left and right. The herati is probably more common in Karabagh than in Senneh and Feraghan where it was also popular. Occasionally these herati rugs have a Savonnerie inspired border, a feature which helps distinguish them. Another distinguishing feature is the choice of colour, which is typically Karabagh i.e. bright red, yellow, pink and light green.

Perhaps the most unusual and charming Karabagh rugs are those with the French Savonnerie floral inspired designs. Originally inspired by Savonnerie rugs brought from Europe by rich merchants in the 18th century, these rugs reflect Western floral designs but in a purely geometric manner. The design has become highly stylised; some have the field completely covered by a repetitive floral motif, while others have a larger repetitive geometric flower posy pattern. In all cases the use of colours is masterly and extremely attractive.

Specification: *Size* – proportionally 5′ 6″ × 7′ 6″ (1·67 × 2·28 m) or 6′ × 16′ (1·83 × 4·88 m) for stair carpets. *Loom* – horizontal. *Warp* – wool. *Weft* – wool. *Pile* – wool, variable in length according to design. *Knot* – Turkish, between 60 and 170 knots per square inch.

Description of plate: Karabagh, wool pile, c. 1900. 6′ 2″ × 3′ 4″ (1·88 × 1·02 m).

131

Kazak

Location of manufacture: Rugs bearing this name come from the highland area of the Caucasus whose centre is the town of Kazak. They are woven by the semi-nomadic shepherds of the region. They are principally antique though a limited number are still made in the area.

General description: Kazak rugs can be easily distinguished both by their distinctive designs and their weave. Weft is always red or brown while the warp is natural. There are always two, three or even more rows of weft threads between every row of knots, which themselves are elongated lengthways. This weaving peculiarity can readily be seen on the back of the rug. The pile is of excellent quality and quite deep. The rugs have earned themselves a reputation of being hardwearing and resistant to damage.

Kazak designs can be identified by their formal nature and their linear quality, both of which are quite distinctive. Popular patterns include the central medallion, multiple medallion, the repeated design, and the 'Eagle Kazak', mention of which has already been made under Karabagh.

Kazaks with the central medallion design have the field taken up by a single octagonal medallion which is contained within a square. Another square, normally accentuated by virtue of a lighter background, is placed within the octagonal medallion. Numerous small geometric motifs including the Caucasian eight-pointed star and rosettes made with geometric squares or rectangles fill the remaining area. The multiple medallion pattern is generally confined to runners or long carpets. In this a row of diamond-shaped medallions run down the centre of the carpet. Each medallion is decorated with the same geometric motif in different colours. In appearance it is similar to the Persian style of Feraghan. Kazaks with the repeated pattern have their field entirely covered by octagons, approximately 8–9 inches (20 cm) in width, each of which has geometric shapes, the outermost one normally consisting of a hooked Greek key. Each octagon is worked in a different combination of colours. The pattern is found both on long and short rugs.

'Eagle Kazaks' or Chelaberd is now also associated with Karabagh, and separation between the two is only possible by careful examination of the weaving characteristics, which can clearly be seen on the back of the rug. The design itself takes the form of large geometric medallions within the form of a cross, two arms of which are of equal length and which end in a point. The motif is dark in colour outlined by an irregular white motif. The remaining field is covered with typical Caucasian geometric motifs.

Specification: *Size* – various, from about 2′ × 3′ 6″ (0·61 × 1·06 m) (or 4′ 6″) (1·37 m) to 5′ × 7′ (1·52 × 2·13 m), and long runners. *Loom* – horizontal. *Warp* – wool. *Weft* – wool, dyed red or brown, 2 or 3 rows after every row of knots. *Pile* – wool, deep. *Knot* – Turkish, fairly low density from 50 – 100 knots per square inch. *Motifs* – formal, geometric, central medallion, multiple medallion, repeated pattern, 'Eagle'.

Description of plates: *Top*: Kazak, wool pile, mid 19th century. 7′ 5″ × 6′ 0″ (2·26 × 1·83 m). *Bottom*: Kazak, wool pile, c.1900. 10″ × 3′ 8″ (2·08 × 1·12 m).

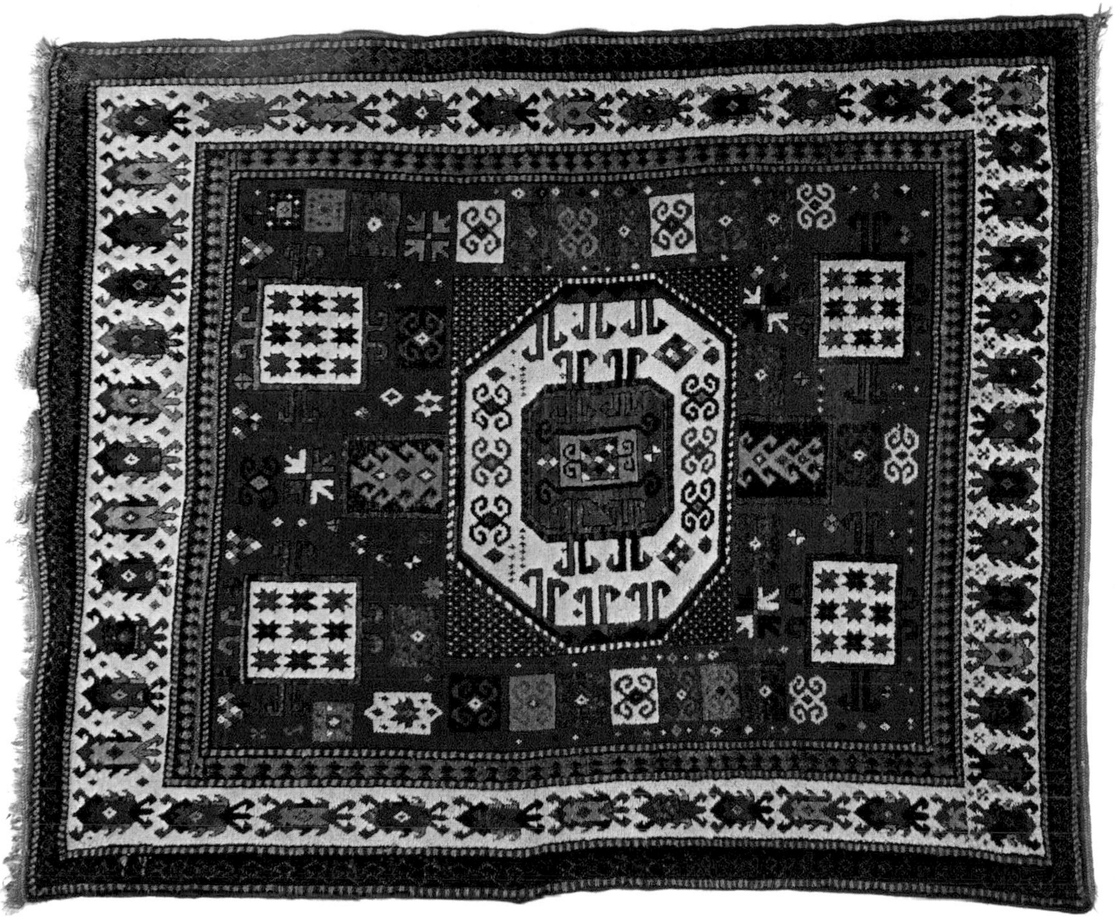

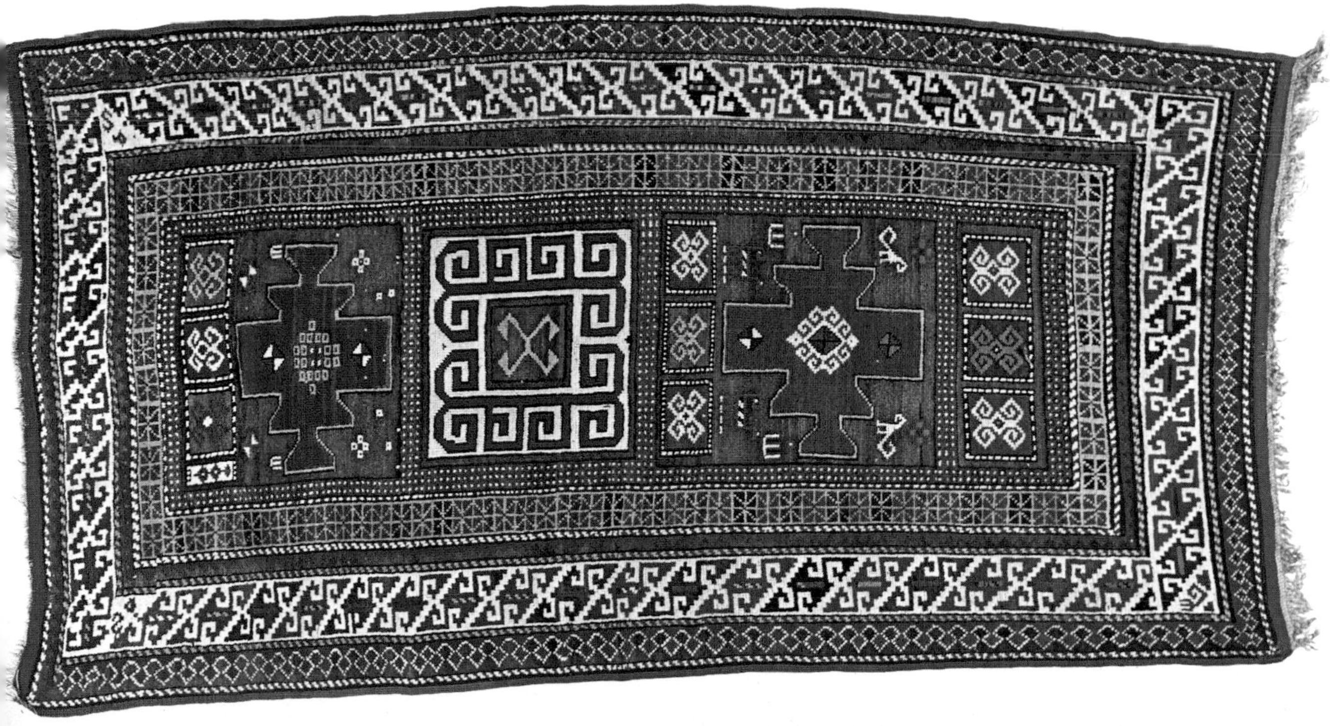

Kuba

Location of manufacture: The town of Kuba is situated in the Caucasus, in the Daghestan district south of the town of Derbend.

General description: An associate group to the Shirvan and Daghestan, the carpets appear to have been woven by Armenians living in the area. Indeed, the so-called 'dragon carpets' were at one time called 'Armenian'. Today they are called Dragon Kuba. These carpets are characterised by what appears to be 'dragons' which run lengthways, between seemingly anthropomorphic linked diamond trellis. The design has strong overtones of the geometric mythical creatures motifs of China, such as the t'ao-t'ieh and kuei dragon. In addition to rugs with this design, rugs were made with other designs similar to Daghestan. One such consists of a central line of alternate squares and rectangles interspaced with animal figures; indeed, animal figures combined with other Caucasian elements is a feature of Kuba rugs. Borders are mostly broad with an 'S' shaped pattern. Colours tend to be red and blue as well as various other striking colours.

Specification: *Size* – between 2′ × 5′ (0·61 × 1·52 m) and 3′ 6″ × 10′ (1·06 × 3·05 m). *Loom* – horizontal. *Warp* – wool. *Weft* – wool (red). *Pile* – wool, deep. *Knot* – Turkish, about 50 – 100 knots per square inch. *Motif* – 'dragon' or as above.

Description of plate: Kuba, 'Perepedil', wool pile, c.1880. 6′ 10″ × 4′ 7″ (2·08 × 1·40 m).

134

Sejur

Location of manufacture: A town in south Caucasus; rugs from this area are generally regarded as a subdivision of the Kuba group.

General description: The characteristic design of Sejur makes these rugs amongst the most attractive of Caucasians. The characteristic pattern is basically quite simple, consisting as it does of three large crosses, running the length of the carpet. These are interspaced with geometric floral designs and surrounded by white borders, which enclose latch-hook or typical Caucasian motifs. The cross motif is usually dark on a natural ground.

The 'St Andrew's' cross motif has extremely ancient origins and can be seen in multiple miniature form in the famous Pazyryk carpet, which was found frozen in a Scythian tomb. In addition to the 'St Andrew's' cross, other designs were also used, usually with a latch-hook border.

Specification: *Size* – Between 2′ × 5′ (0.61 × 1·52 m) and 3′ × 16′ (0·92 × 4·88 m). *Loom* – horizontal. *Warp* – wool. *Weft* – wool. *Pile* – wool, deep. *Knot* – Turkish, about 50–100 knots per square inch. *Motifs* – triple 'St Andrew's' cross and/or latch-hook borders.

Description of plate: Sejur, wool pile, c.1880. 7′ 10″ × 3′ 6″ (2·39 × 1·07 m).

Shirvan

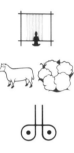

Location of manufacture: The village of this name is situated on the flat plain near the south-west shore of the Caspian Sea. The Shirvan district south of Kuba itself encompasses the southern area of Azerbaijan, including the River Kura.

General description: The large number of Caucasian rugs that could not be attributed easily to other rug-making areas, have been given the name of Shirvan, almost as a label of convenience. This may be due to the fact that, as a geographical area, it has received influences from a number of peoples at different times in its history – testimony to which can be seen in the motifs which are found on true Shirvan rugs. This, however, is no excuse for the use of Shirvan as a label of last resort, for the area has produced designs with distinctive features of their own.

Early in its history it came under the influence of Persia and naturally absorbed Persian designs. From these floral motifs developed the harshang or crab-motif, a design which although now formal and stylised, almost certainly developed from Persian inspired floral motifs. The design is employed in Shirvan rugs as lines of crab-like flowers, completely covering the field. Borders may also be harshang or what is known as kufic, i.e. that in form it resembles the kufic script.

Stylisation is everywhere – both of floral and animal figures. Another design employs a line of various geometric motifs, eight-pointed stars, rosettes etc., surrounded by a field of stylised flowers and animals. The border normally consists of the serrated leaf pattern. Prayer rugs are also found.

Colours are varied, normally bright with darker, more subdued backgrounds, and with white occurring especially in borders. Blue is often predominant in early rugs.

Specification: *Size* – variable, but generally between 2′ × 5′ (0·61 × 1·52 m) and 3′ 6″ × 16′ (1·06 × 4·88 m). *Loom* – vertical. *Warp* – wool (old) or wool and cotton from about 1850 to 1920. Modern warps are cotton. *Weft* – same as warp. *Pile* – wool, close-cropped. *Knot* – Turkish, density from about 100 to 200 knots per square inch. *Motifs* – as above.

Description of plate: Shirvan, wool pile, c.1900. 5′ 0″ × 2′ 7″ (1·52 × 0·79 m).

139

Sumac

Location of manufacture: The town of Shemakha is situated some 30 miles (48 km) from the Russian port of Baku on the Caspian Sea. Sumac (Shemakha) has given its name to the rugs, which not only come from the town itself but from Sile and Verne and a large area around, including Azerbaijan and south Daghestan. From the 9th to 16th centuries Sumac was the residence of the Shirvan shahs.

General description: Although typically Caucasian in inspiration and extremely geometric in design, they differ radically from other Caucasian rugs, in that they are woven but have no knotted pile. In this respect they are similar to some of the kelims of Senneh. This weft face technique was once widely spread, but is today restricted to one or two centres.

In this type of rug there are two weft threads, both of which are wool, as is the warp. One of the wefts performs the normal function of providing the basic structure of the rug, while the second, which is coloured and produces the design, is wrapped around the top, woven in and out as in a chain stitch. New colours are introduced in line where they are needed, from the back of the rug. Contrary to what might be expected, Sumac rugs are very strong.

In one popular pattern, the field is normally composed of geometric patterns of diamonds containing rosettes or eight-pointed stars. This may be large, with three or more occupying the entire centre of the rug, but there are a number of variations both large and small. A feature of the borders is that there is almost always an outer band of hooked Greek key or latch design. The field is often a dull red, with motifs in bright colours; the large diamonds mentioned above are more often than not dark blue. There are a number of different patterns and colours, all of which are rigidly geometric.

Specification: *Size* – from very small items to rugs ranging from about 5′ × 8′ (1·52 × 2·44 m) to 6′ 6″ × 9′ 6″ (1·98 × 2·89 m). *Loom* – vertical. *Warp* – wool. *Weft* – wool. No knotted pile. *Motifs* – geometric.

Description of plate: Sumac, Verne, brocaded cover, wool, plain weave, mid 19th century. 6′ 2″ × 6′ 5″ (1·88 × 1·96 m), woven in two sections.

140

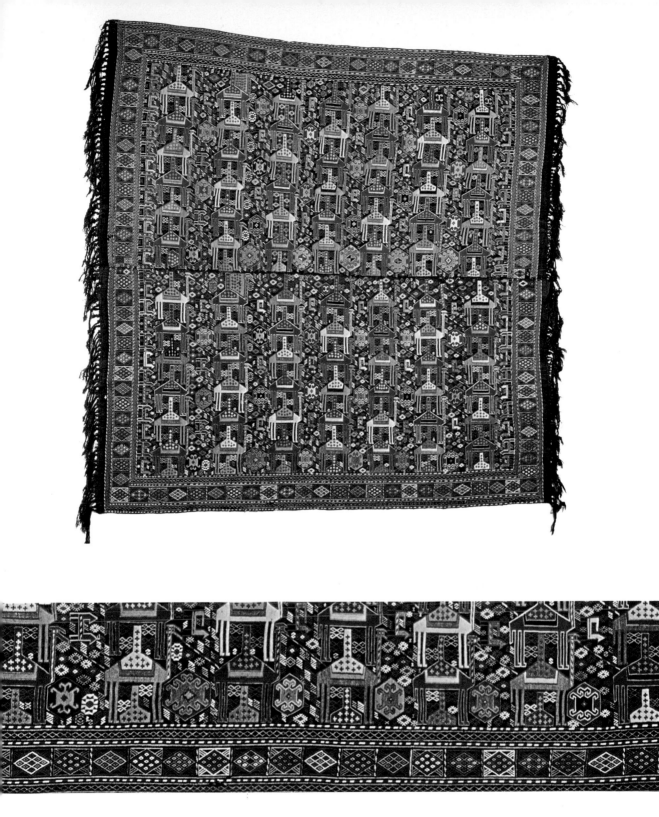

Talish

Location of manufacture: The Talish mountain region, from whence these rugs come, is situated in the southern Caucasus, north of the town of Ardebil in Iran.

General description: These thick pile rugs belong to the Shirvan group. They are almost invariably runners. The field is normally red or blue and may be plain, divided into squares, or covered with diamonds and squares or circular motifs, a design which may be repeated on the border, interspersed between four small squares or diamonds. The wool is of good quality.

Specification: *Size* – mainly runners. *Loom* – vertical. *Warp* – wool. *Weft* – wool. *Pile* – wool. *Knot* – Turkish, about 100 – 200 knots per square inch. *Motifs* – geometric.

Description of plate: Talish runner, wool pile, c. 1860. 9′ 5″ × 3′ 8″ (2·87 × 1·12 m).

Afghan

Location of manufacture: Rugs bearing the general label 'Afghan' in fact come from a large area of Afghanistan. They are also of two kinds, the 'old', woven by nomadic Turkomans, and the 'new', woven in craft centres by Turkomans and Afghans. Some Afghan rugs look very similar to Turkoman. Rugs were, and still are, collected together at Herat and Kabul.

General description: Old Afghans are almost copper in colour, with designs worked in dark blue, which appears almost black. They have a short pile with a fairly high density of knots. More modern examples are easily distinguished by their rich warm dark red, which, when combined with dark blue, brown and black used in the patterns, is quite unmistakable. White and yellow are also occasionally present on some rugs. The principal motif is the large gul, which is arranged in lines, normally two in number, separated by stylised branches. These guls are formed by an octagon, which encloses a central square and which, apart from the square, is divided into four sections each of which encloses the same pattern, alternatively in positive and negative. The wide border is normally formed by a number of narrow geometric borders, which include serrated leaf and hooked Greek key or latch designs. The gul design is similar to Bukhara.

Specification: *Size* – variable, between 7′ × 10′ (2·13 × 3·05 m) and 9′ × 12′ (2·74 × 3·66 m). *Loom* – vertical. *Warp* – wool (occasionally goat's). *Weft* – wool (occasionally goat's). *Pile* – good quality wool. *Knot* – Persian, between 60 and 180 knots per square inch. *Motifs* – Afghan guls, similar to Bukhara.

Description of plate: Afghan, wool and silk pile, late 19th century. 4′ 9″ × 4′ 0″ (1·45 × 1·22 m).

145

Baluchi

Location of manufacture: Baluchi rugs are the handiwork of the Baluchi tribe, a nomadic tribe that inhabit an area spanning N.E. Iran, Afghanistan and Baluchistan. Some rugs are said to be woven in the town of Firdaus in central Khorasan, by weavers of Arab origin.

General description: There are basically two kinds of Baluchi rugs, those marketed in the Iranian town of Meshed and known as Meshed-Baluchi, and those marketed through Afghanistan, in particular the town of Herat. Nowadays there is a modern Baluchi which is shipped to world markets through the port of Karachi in Pakistan.

Many Baluchi rugs are prayer mats, but other types are also made. Colours are rich with red and blue predominating and are somewhat similar to Afghans. White is also a feature. Designs are formal. There are numerous patterns which differ from rug to rug. In prayer rugs a 'tree of life' often occupies the mihrab. Many of the designs are not indigenous but have been borrowed from other centres in Iran and the Caucasus. They nevertheless have the typical formality of form found on all Baluchi rugs. Amongst these motifs may be mentioned the Bukhara gul. The borders are formed by narrow bands, one of which is wider than the next and is the same colour as the main ground. Designs are geometric.

Colour is most distinctive in Baluchi rugs – nearly all follow the same colour scheme, the exception being when a natural camel beige ground is used.

Specification: *Size* – normally small, especially prayer rugs – from 2′ 6″ × 4′ 6″ (0·76 × 1·37 m). *Loom* – horizontal. *Warp* – wool. *Weft* – wool. *Pile* – good quality wool but not deep, (sometimes mixed with cotton). *Knot* – Persian, from about 50 – 100 knots per square inch.

Description of plates: *Left*: Baluchi bag, wool pile, c.1920. *Right*: Baluchi, wool and white cotton pile, c.1900. 6′ 9″ × 3′ 2″ (2·06 × 0·97 m).

Beshir

Location of manufacture: Rugs with this name are the handiwork of the Beshir tribe, a Turkoman nomadic tribe, who now live in the area about 125 miles (201 km) south of Bukhara centred on the town of Beshir, near the Amu Darya River. The tribe is found in a border region touching Uzbekistan, Turkmenistan and Afghanistan. The town of Beshir is probably the marketing centre for the rugs.

General description: Beshir rugs differ markedly from other Turkoman rugs in that the designs are usually much smaller, closer together and less geometric and formal They often appear to be red, but in these cases close examination will reveal that this overall colour is the result of the closeness of red decoration, which overpowers the blue ground. A vivid yellow is also a feature. The rugs are normally quite large and covered with numerous interconnecting small motifs with floral overtones. Common elements are the lozenge, the herati, palmettes, rosettes, octagons, leaves and stars. The borders vary and can reflect the central design, or be composed of numerous narrow bands of small geometric shapes.

Specification: *Size* – large, some up to about 25 feet (7·62 m) long. *Loom* – horizontal. *Warp* – wool. *Weft* – wool, two rows between every row of knots. *Pile* – wool, fairly deep (sometimes mixed with silk). *Knot* – Persian (though sometimes Turkish), 50 – 150 knots per square inch.

Description of plate: Beshir, Juval (Bag face), wool and silk pile, 19th century. 6′ 1″ × 3′ 8″ (1·85 × 1·12 m).

148

149

Salor

Location of manufacture: The Salor were at one time the dominant tribe of the Turkomans. They lived on the shores of the Caspian Sea, but due to a change in fortune and pressure from other tribes, moved southwards into Iran.

General description: Rugs bearing this name are either antique, made during the first half of the 19th century, or simply rugs with Salor inspired designs, for after a severe campaign against them by Abbas Mirza in 1831, their way of life seems to have been made so difficult that they gave up weaving. This theory is backed up by a study of weave patterns; however rugs bearing Salor designs still tend to be called Salor.

Designs tend to be based on the octagonal gul, usually in rows with the tarantula pattern. Colours are normally red, ranging from a browny-red to copper, with the details in brown, black, white or yellow. Some have a cream ground, but these are rare.

Specification: *Size* – variable. *Loom* – horizontal. *Warp* – wool. *Weft* – wool. *Pile* – wool, good quality. *Knot* – Persian, between 80 – 200 knots per square inch. *Motifs* – Turkoman guls, tarantulas etc.

Description of plate: Salor, Turkoman, wool pile, c.1920. 6′ 6″ × 3′ 8″ (1·98 × 1·12 m).

Tekke

Location of manufacture: The Tekke is the largest nomadic Turkoman tribe and is believed to be originally an offshoot of the Salor. In this respect they have not only retained the Salor ability for weaving, but improved upon it, for their rugs are perhaps the finest of the Turkomans. They are fairly widely spread, living in an area around Merv and Ashkhabad and north-west Afghanistan.

General description: Tekke rugs and carpets are extremely attractive and have long been a favourite in Europe. Many rugs simply labelled as Turkoman may well have been made by the Tekke. Compared with the Yomud their rugs are finer, knotting denser and designs more accurate. The tribe was originally widely spread, sometimes separated by other tribes, a fact that might well explain the presence of two weaving patterns. One is fairly easy to recognise with its warp arranged in pairs in regular parallel lines.

The octagonal gul is common, with the areas in between linked with hooks, stars or tarantula patterns. The colours are warm and somewhat lighter than the Yomud.

Many of the so-called Bukhara rugs are the work of the Tekke. They are called such, it is thought, because the carpets and rugs were marketed in the famous bazaar at Bukhara, which is situated on the border of Turkmenistan and Uzbekistan. Tekke Bukharas are quality rugs, hardwearing, yet with a soft silky pile. They are simple in design yet extremely attractive. The typical motif is the Bukhara gul, or octagon with slightly rounded sides, which is made up from rectangles arranged to produce a star shape. These guls are linked with each other by lines, which intersect the guls forming a grid. Each section of the gul alternates in colour. The area between the guls is normally filled with four-pointed stars. The borders are composed of three bands, two narrow and a wide central band, which is normally formed of octagons of varying colour combinations. The border at the head of the rug is normally decorated with diagonally arranged serrated leaves. Colours tend to be red, blue, orange, black, green and ivory.

Specification: *Size* – most sizes. *Loom* – horizontal. *Warp* – wool. *Weft* – wool, sometimes double. *Pile* – good quality, silky wool. *Knot* – Persian, from about 150 – 300 knots per square inch. *Motifs* – gul, especially Bukhara.

Description of plate: Tekke, wool pile, c.1900. 5′ 6″ × 3′ 0″ (1·68 × 0·92 m).

152

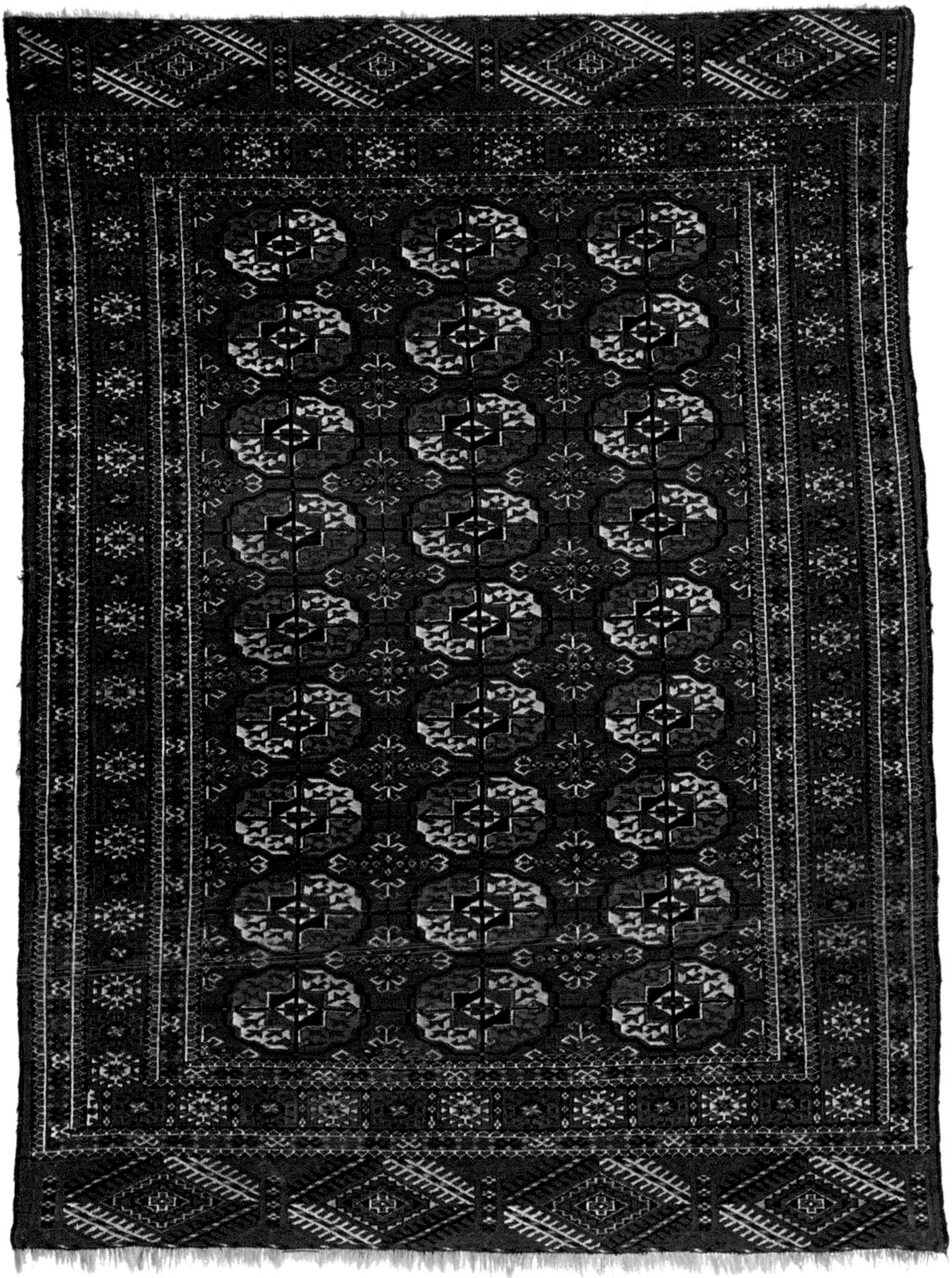

Description of plate: Tekke, (hatchli), wool pile, c.1900. 4′0″ × 3′6″ (1·22 × 1·07 m). The Hatchli design is frequently found in Turkoman carpets. It comes from an Armenian word meaning cross – for the design in the centre of the field is divided into four by a cross band. It may represent a wooden door.

Ersari

Location of manufacture: Rugs labelled Ersari generally come from north-east Afghanistan.

General Description: The Ersari are a Turkoman tribe who may be related to the Beshir and Kizyl-Ayak. Designs tend not to be distinctive.

Specification: As for other Turkoman rugs.

Description of plate: Ersari, Engsi (hatchli), wool pile, 19th century. 5′6″ × 4′11″ (1·68 × 1·50 m).

155

Uzbek

Location of manufacture: A Central Asian tribe, unrelated to the Turkoman.

General description: Although the Uzbeks are thought to have produced pile rugs, in the West virtually no examples have been able to be positively attributed to them. They are principally known for their superb embroideries, known as 'suzanis' and 'ikat' textiles. The former are very beautiful, being worked in attractive bright colours.

Specification: *Size* – various. *Embroidery, face* – silk.

Description of plate: Uzbek Suzani, silk embroidered cover. West Turkmenistan, c.1890. 5′4″ × 4′2″ (1·63 × 1·07 m).

Yomud

Location of manufacture: Rugs of this name are the work of a nomad Turkoman tribe of that name. At one time they lived by the Atrek and Gorgan rivers near the south-eastern edge of the Caspian Sea, but today they are more widely spread and the Yomud mainly live in north-east Iran.

General description: The name Yomud encompasses a varied group of rugs and it is far from certain that all bearing the name were actually made by the tribe. They may well be the work of associated tribes such as the Igdyr, Ogurjalis, Aba, Abdal or Arabatchi. It is possible to distinguish two distinct types of weaving in this group. In one the knots are evenly spread on the same plane, while in the other more common weave the warp is prominent giving the weave a rigid appearance. A common design consists of rows of interconnected diamond-shaped guls, with broad borders. Colours tend to be dark red and range to maroon and purple, with highlights in white, green or yellow. Certain types of Bukhara (with Bukhara gul) carpets are woven by the Yomud.

Specification: *Size* – variable, in most sizes. *Loom* – horizontal. *Warp* – wool. *Weft* – wool. *Pile* – good quality wool, sometimes with silk. *Knot* – Persian between 150 and 300 knots per square inch. *Motif* – various, including interconnecting diamonds or trellis, Bukhara guls.

Description of plate: Yomund, Engsi (hatchli), wool pile, c.1900. 5′5″ × 4′0″ (1·65 × 1·22 m).

India

Indo-Persian (Isfahan)

Location of manufacture: A number of centres in India were responsible in the 17th and 18th centuries for making rugs in the Persian tradition. Among these were Agra, Fatehpur-Sikri and Lahore.

General description: In the 16th century the Moghul emperor Akbar brought a number of carpet weavers to India from Persia and set up an imperial 'factory' at Lahore. It is possible that a number of these weavers were from Isfahan, as Indo-Persian carpets clearly reflect the designs and techniques of the Persian centre. Other designs come from Herat. Indo-Persian rugs are amongst the finest of antique rugs. Their reputation was high throughout Europe. One of the first Europeans to own one was the ambassador of James I to the court of the Moghul emperor Jehangir, Sir Thomas Roe. Others were made for the Director of the East India Company, Sir John Wolsten Holme. One of the finest surviving examples can be seen today at Girdlers' Hall, London. It was ordered in 1630 by Sir John Bell as a gift for the Girdlers' Company. It was presented to them in 1634 and still hangs in their hall.

These early Indian carpets were extremely fine, especially those made of silk. Some of the finest have a knot density of 2500 to the square inch! Even some of their woollen rugs have up to 1200 knots per square inch – this was achieved by tying fine wool on silk warps.

As the fame and success of Indian rugs spread, workshops were set up in many other parts of India. The East India Company too established 'factories' as did the French, who started a small workshop in Pondicherri in 1702.

Indian carpets are of high quality. Today, after a decline in quality after the Second World War, they have greatly improved and are of high quality. Most of the designs of the early rugs were Persian, but later on European and other elements were introduced to satisfy market demand.

Specification: *Size* – variable. *Loom* – vertical. *Warp* – Silk or cotton. *Weft* – silk or cotton. *Pile* – wool or silk. *Knot* – Persian, varying in density, up to 2500 knots per square inch in silk rugs. *Motifs* – Persian.

Description of plate: Indo-Persian, wool pile, c.1900. 4′ 9″ × 3′ 2″ (1·45 × 0·97 m).

Kashmir

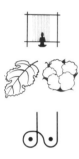

Location of manufacture: At one time an independent state, Kashmir is now split between Pakistan and India. The main centre of carpet manufacture was and is Srinagar.

General description: Carpets were first made in Kashmir as early as the 15th century, when a factory was established under the patronage of Prince Shahi Khan. These workshops continued to make carpets until the middle of the 18th century, when they closed down seemingly due to lack of demand. However, they lost demand for only a short time, as new workshops were established in Srinagar under German management, the factory eventually being taken over by The East India Carpet Company. As Kashmir developed its good name for rugs and carpets, so other workshops were opened. Today some very fine rugs are still made there.

Designs tend to be adapted from various sources, especially Persian. Kashmir 'Bukhara' were and still are made. Some of the finest rugs have as many as 2000 knots per square inch. Kashmir is also known for a kind of chain stitch rug.

Specification: *Size* – ranging from small prayer rugs to full size carpets. *Loom* – vertical. *Warp* – cotton – silk. *Weft* – cotton – silk. *Pile* – wool or silk. *Knot* – Persian, varying density according to quality, can be as high as 2000 knots per square inch.

Description of plate: Kashmir, wool pile, c.1920. 6′ 1″ × 4′ 6″ (2·00 × 1·38 m).

Description of plate: *Top left*: A group of patterns and designs used in making Kashmir rugs. The coloured pattern on the left is an original design of the East India Carpet Company. The bundle on the right is a weaving pattern for an entire carpet; the strips of paper are threaded onto the warp and give detailed design instructions to the weavers.

Top right: Weaving a Kashmir rug – often a whole family is employed for months, even years, on the production of one rug.

Bottom left: After the rug is taken off the loom, it is cut and brushed.

Bottom right: The finishing touches being made to a new Kashmir wool rug.

Description of plate: The finest rugs have hundreds of knots to the square inch. Children are often employed in this work as their hands can best deal with the minute knots. Here, an eight-year-old Kashmiri boy is working on an intricate design.

China

Location of manufacture: Unlike the carpets of Persia, Turkey, the Caucasus and other centres, Chinese carpets cannot be attributed to any particular region of China. This is due to an over-all similarity of technique and choice of designs.

General description: In the same way that it is generally impossible to determine with accuracy the location of manufacture of Chinese carpets, so it is with making accurate assessments of age. Techniques have generally remained the same, and designs have, like those used in other Chinese arts, been utilised in many different periods. In spite of this, it is possible to make some reasonable attributions based on condition, materials and other elements. In this respect experience in seeing as many specimens as possible is the best help.

The main centres of carpet production were in Sinkiang, Peking and Tientsin. In design they can be divided into those of traditional inspiration and those of Western inspiration. Traditional design elements include Buddhist and Taoist elements, dragons, cloud motifs and auspicious symbols. There are a number of border designs, some ancient in origin but which sometimes look European. Rugs produced in Sinkiang often have Caucasian overtones. Rugs with Western inspired designs are

Description of plate: Chinese, wool pile, 19th century. 3′ 2″ × 2′ 0″ (0·97 × 0·61 m).

Description of plate: Chinese, chair cover, wool pile. 19th century. 2′ 6″ × 2′ 3″ (0·76 × 0·69 m).

mainly floral in nature after French Aubusson patterns. These rugs and carpets have delicate pastel coloured floral decoration arranged in elaborate central medallions or borders, or with a predominantly plain field with spring floral decoration. The effect of most carpets both traditional and Western is the special cutting technique of the pile which emphasises the pattern.

Specification: *Size* – variable. *Loom* – vertical. *Warp* – cotton (thick). *Weft* – cotton (thick). *Pile* – good quality wool – soft and somewhat fragile. *Knot* – mainly Persian though Turkish is occasionally found, low density of about 30 – 50 knots per square inch. *Motifs* – as above.

Description of plate: Chinese saddle rug, wool pile, 19th century.

Dragon medallion

Description of plate. *Top left*: China, wool pile, 18th century. Detail of rug showing the geometric central floral medallion on a rice pattern background. The colours are now faded but were originally yellow and green, with blue and white details.

Top right: China, wool pile, late 18th century. Detail of a rug showing floral medallion in white and shades of blue on gold.

Bottom left: China, wool pile, 19th century. Detail of rug showing a central floral and geometric medallion, flanked each end by flowers in vases and pots, executed in shades of blue on a cream ground. The design, within a rectangular border of key and dot motifs, is surrounded by pairs of small floral motifs.

Bottom right: China, wool pile, 19th century. Detail of rug. A central medallion is surrounded by flowers in vases. The design is executed in blues, gold and cream, on a dark blue ground.

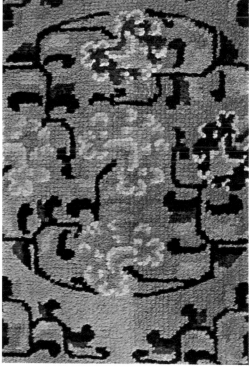

Tibet

Location of manufacture: Tibetan rugs are principally the work of nomad and small village workshops. They were made all over Tibet as well as in the Himalayan states of Ladakh, Sikkim and Bhutan and in Nepal. Since 1952 with the large number of refugees settling in the Himalayas outside Tibet, production has increased in these centres.

General description: The rugs are on the whole coarse and rather bright in colour. They are also small in size. Designs are similar in some respects to Chinese rugs especially from the border areas of Manchuria. The motifs are Buddhist in inspiration in particular, Lamaistic, i.e. the Buddhist sect of Tibet. In addition to the Buddhist emblems of China, symbols such as the vajra (thunderbolt) either single or crossed is found, and the sacred vase. These designs are used on both domestic and temple rugs and cushions as well as on saddle cloths. The symmetrical (Ghiordes) knot is used. It is extremely difficult to date Tibetan rugs accurately as they often appear much older than they really are. They are also often discoloured by the smoke of butterlamps.

Specification: *Size* – generally small. *Loom* – both horizontal and small vertical. *Warp* – wool, sometimes cotton. *Weft* – wool, sometimes cotton. *Pile* – thick wool. *Knot* – Turkish, low density about 50 knots to the square inch. *Motifs* – Buddhist including Lamaist symbols.

Description of plate: Tibetan – wool pile, c.1890. 4′ 10″ × 3′ 0″ (1·48 × 0·92 m).

173

Vajra or thunderbolt motif

Dragon motif

Description of plate: Tibet, wool pile, c.1925. 4′ × 2′ (1·22 × 0·61 m). Floral and Buddhist motif in typical Tibetan colours. Three central floral medallions enclosed by a rectangle of key motifs. The rug has been bound to prevent fraying. Also shown is a detail of the front and back of the same rug, which shows the coarse knots.

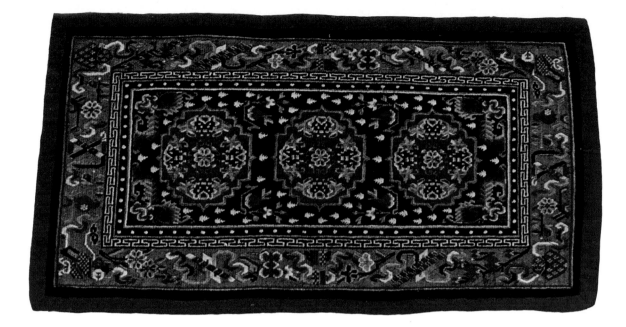

OTHER RUG MAKING CENTRES

Persian

Ardebil

Location of manufacture: The village of Ardebil is situated in the Azerbaijan mountains on the border of Iran and the Caucasus.

General description: One of the most famous antique Persian carpets, the 16th century Ardebil carpet in the Victoria and Albert Museum, London, and its sister in the Los Angeles County Museum of Art, is named after this village where it was discovered. It was not made there, however, most likely coming originally from Kashan. Ardebil rugs, in fact, do not look anything like this majestic ancestor, for they take their inspiration from the adjoining Caucasus, in particular Shirvan, but are distinguishable from rugs from this Caucasian centre by virtue of the fact that the wool is coarser, and by Ardebil's unique colour scheme, based on the striking use of bright reds and green on a light ivory field. The border of Ardebil rugs too is different, in that it is much more elaborate, made up of a central border of octagons and geometric rosettes flanked by narrow guards. The design itself more often than not consists of three diamonds running down the centre surrounded by various Caucasian motifs.

Specification: *Size* – generally not large, averaging around 4′ 9″ × 7′ 3″ (1·43 × 2·21 m). *Loom* – vertical. *Warp* – cotton, occasionally wool. *Weft* – cotton, occasionally wool. *Pile* – wool. *Knot* – Turkish, between 50 and 120 knots per square inch. *Motifs* – Caucasian.

Joshaqan

Location of manufacture: The village lies in mountainous country in central Iran, north of Isfahan.

General description: Rugs have been made in the village for over two hundred years, during which period the designs have changed little. A characteristic feature of these rugs is that the design, which is principally floral, has its stylised motifs arranged on the field as diamonds which cover the whole field. Some carpets have diamond-shaped medallions outlined with a white Greek key motif, within which are the same diamond assemblies of stylised flowers.

Specification: *Size* – various, but generally small. *Loom* – vertical. *Warp* – cotton. *Weft* – cotton. *Pile* – wool, medium. *Knot* – Persian with a density of 60 to 180 knots per square inch.

Karaj

Location of manufacture: The village of Karaj where these rugs are made lies north-east of Tabriz.

General description: The rugs are similar in many respects to those of Tabriz but are woven from superior wool which tends to give them a finer, more uniform pile. Their design is quite distinctive and easily recognisable, consisting generally of a large central diamond-shaped medallion flanked on either side by medallions of the same colour, but normally star-shaped. The medallions and the field are covered with geometric plant motifs. Colours are sober and include dark blue, red, yellow and green.

Specification: As for Tabriz, with the exception that the warp is single.

Mehriban

Location of manufacture: A village in N. Iran, the details are similar to those for Heriz. Another rug also marketed under this name is quite different, and comes from a village in north Iran, north-west of Hamadan.

Meshkin

Location of manufacture: The village is on the frontier between Iran and the Caucasus.

General description: Similar to Sarab and Ardebil rugs, they have however weft and warp of wool. The pile is fine quality.

Specification: As Ardebil rugs, but always with weft and warp of wool.

Mir

Location of manufacture: Probably woven in the district of Seraband at the village of Mal-e-Mir.

General description: Ancestor of Seraband rugs, similar in design but of much finer quality. The field is normally blue, with the striking use of rich yellow in the design.

Mosul

See Hamadan.

Nain

Location of manufacture: Rugs of this name are made in the town of Nain in central Iran, near the rugged uplands. It is near Isfahan.

General description: These rugs are fairly recent in origin, the oldest belonging to the early 20th century. Quite distinguishable, they often have the field of cream or other light colour, or red. The decoration is similar to some Isfahans and is floral or faunal in inspiration.

Specification: *Size* – most sizes. *Loom* – vertical. *Warp* – cotton. *Weft* – cotton, double row between knots. *Pile* – wool, sometimes with silk, occasionally entirely of silk. *Knot* – Persian high density between 300 – 600 knots per square inch. *Motifs* – similar to Isfahan.

Seraband

Location of manufacture: Seraband rugs come from a number of villages in the mountainous area of south of Arak in western Iran, which has itself in the past made rugs bearing this name.

General description: The descendant of the almost legendary Mir carpets. The Mir-boteh motif employed by Mir is also present on Seraband rugs. The boteh motif covers the entire central field, or occasionally is within a diamond central medallion. The field can be blue as in Mir, ivory, red or even pink. Geometric and boteh motifs are used as borders, also a red 'Seraband' border.

Specification: *Size* – various, but especially runners. *Loom* – vertical. *Warp* – coarse cotton, sometimes dyed a light blue, two warp threads between knots (see reverse of rug). *Weft* – coarse cotton. *Pile* – wool. *Knot* – Turkish, about 100 knots to the square inch. *Motifs* – Mir-boteh.

Tehran

Location of manufacture: Capital of Iran.

General description: The ancestor of Veramin and as such the designs are in some respects similar.

Veramin

Location of manufacture: A town some 32 miles (52 km) south of Tehran.

General description: Rugs with this name do not have a long ancestry, and date only from the end of the 19th century. They are thought to be made by Pazekis, a tribe of Kurdish descent. There are two types of Veramin rugs, those made in the town and those made in the outlying villages. They can be distinguished by their weave, for the urban weave has an unusual characterisic of having two wefts, one of which is light blue. Designs tend to be either floral or faunal almost as in Persian miniature paintings or the zel-i-sultan or Mina Khani motifs. The borders normally echo the central field design, formed of diamond and solid triangle point to point. Field colours are various but especially dark blue or red.

Specification: *Size* – various, proportionally about 7′ × 10′ 6″ (2·13 × 3·20 m). *Loom* – vertical. *Warp* – cotton. *Weft* – cotton, in town rugs, double, one thread dyed light blue. *Pile* – wool. *Knot* – Persian, between 200 – 300 knots per square inch.

Anatolian

Isparta

Location of manufacture: A town south-west of Konya.

General description: Rugs of this name have sometimes been marketed as Smyrna. They are similar to the rugs of Tabriz, but can be distinguished by virtue of the paler colour and by the general limpness of the rug. Mainly modern, from the beginning of the 20th century.

Specification: *Size* – various. *Loom* – vertical. *Warp* – cotton. *Weft* – cotton. *Pile* – wool. *Knot* – Turkish, low density.

Kayseri

Location of manufacture: The town of Kayseri is situated in central Turkey. The capital of a province of the same name, it has been famous as a rug-making centre for centuries. Marco Polo mentions the rugs he saw there on his travels in 1271. In spite of this early tradition, the quality of rug weaving has deteriorated over the years, but the quality is still superior to many, especially to Sivas, with which it can be grouped. It is notable for its silk rugs. There are no particular patterns peculiar to Kayseri.

Specification: Similar to Sivas, with the exception of silk pile rugs, which are high in density.

Kirshehir

Location of manufacture: The town is capital of the province of the same name.

General description: Similar in character to Mudjur (see Mudjur). Colours, however, are somewhat paler. Prayer rugs too are more common to Kirshehir.

Specification: See Mudjur.

Kula

Location of manufacture: The village is in eastern Anatolia, south of Kayseri.

General description: Rugs from Kula are very similar in many respects to Ghiordes and it is often very difficult to tell them apart. Some Kula rugs have prefixes which indicate their design. They are; Komarlu, a rug in which the field is worked in very dark sombre colour; Mazerlik, or graveyard Kulas. The latter are so-named because the rug has a vertically framed decoration of cypress trees and houses on a cherry red field. These may have been used to carry the dead to the cemetery, but this use is unconfirmed and uncertain. Kula prayer rugs are similar to Ghiordes but often the mihrab is small and covered with decorative motifs.

Specification: *Size* – generally small in size and elongated. *Loom* – vertical. *Warp* – double wool, sometimes cotton. *Weft* – wool, sometimes cotton, rarely jute. *Pile* – good quality wool. *Knot* – Turkish, between 40 and 80 knots per square inch. *Motifs* – Komarlu (dark), Mazerlik, cemetery.

Ladik

Location of manufacture: A small town situated a short distance north-west of Konya.

General description: Early Ladik rugs are amongst the finest of antique Turkish rugs. They have over the years somewhat declined in quality but those of the 19th century are still of good quality. The rug-weaving centre of Konya, although having an older tradition than Ladik, in fact copied some Ladik designs.

The Ladik prayer rug design is quite distinctive – the central mihrab is surrounded by a wide border, having geometric tulips and rosettes, flanked by narrow guards. The mihrab itself is divided from the rest of the field by a narrow line or Greek key pattern. At the base of the mihrab are large stylised tulips.

Specification: *Size* – small to medium. *Loom* – vertical. *Warp* – wool. *Weft* – wool. *Pile* – good quality wool. *Knot* – Turkish, from 60 to 120 knots per square inch.

Sivas

Location of manufacture: A town in central Turkey, the capital of the province of the same name.

General description: Antique Sivas are fine rugs but unfortunately the modern product which is marketed under the same name is very inferior. The designs are not Turkish but Persian, resembling Tabriz. They are however, inferior to Tabriz.

Specification: *Size* – fairly large, averaging 8′ × 12′ (2·44 × 3·66 m). *Loom* – vertical. *Warp* – cotton. *Weft* – cotton. *Pile* – wool. *Knot* – Turkish, low density between 50 and 70 knots per square inch. Good antique specimens have as many as 300 knots to the square inch.

Smyrna

Location of manufacture: Rugs bearing this name come from the part of Izmir on the Aegean coast of Turkey.

General description: The town of Smyrna (modern day Izmir) was a major collecting and exporting centre for rugs and thus rugs bearing this name may come from areas some distance away. In fact some have used the name wrongly to indicate 'Turkish'. These rugs are generally of poor quality, having inferior wool and a low density of knotting.

Ushak

Location of manufacture: A town east of Ghiordes and north of Kula.

General description: Rugs from Ushak were particularly famous in the 15th and 17th centuries in Europe, and are often depicted in paintings of the period. A typical example is the Star Ushak rug. Rugs of the 19th century and later are inferior with low density knotting.

Specification: For 19th century and later, similar to Sivas.

Yahyali

Location of manufacture: The village is in eastern Anatolia, south of Kayseri.

General description: Similar to Yuruk, the designs are slightly different in that the number of hexagons in the central medallion is reduced to as low as two.

Specification: Similar to Yuruk.

Yuruk

Location of manufacture: Anatolian rugs made by nomads of various provenance.

General description: The term Yuruk is vague, and it is applied to rugs whose provenance cannot be more accurately described. Thus sometimes the name precedes another, which means a nomad rug of such-and-such a design. The designs are geometric and very similar to Caucasian. A common design is a large central hexagon in which a number of other hexagons are enclosed, all with variations in outline, such as serrated edges, hooked and stepped. The remaining field is covered by rosettes and eight-pointed stars while the border is normally a serrated leaf design.

Specification: *Size* – generally small. *Loom* – horizontal. *Warp* – wool. *Weft* – wool. *Pile* – wool. *Knot* – Turkish, low in density, about 50–100 knots per square inch. *Motifs* – geometric. Similar to Caucasian.

Caucasian

Derbend

Location of manufacture: A town on the west of the Caspian Sea in Daghestan.

General description: These rugs are generally poor quality Daghestans made during the last hundred years or so. For description, see Daghestan.

Specification: Similar to Daghestan, but inferior in quality. Urbanised production with vertical looms.

Turkoman

Bukhara

Location of manufacture: The city of Bukhara, on the border of Turkmenistan and Uzbekistan.

General description: Bukhara was a major marketing centre for the rugs of the Turkoman tribes, and thus over the years many of the rugs have been wrongly labelled with the name of the city. Today it is becoming more acceptable to describe the rugs with their individual tribal names such as Tekke, Salor, Yomud, Saruq, etc. The typical design is the gul.

Specification: As for Turkoman tribes, see individual specification.

Kerki

Location of manufacture: Area of Bukhara.

General description: As for Turkoman, special design of gul which is formalised and which covers the entire field. See *Designs and Motifs*.

Kizyl-Ayak

Location of manufacture: Area of Bukhara.
General description: Distinctive gul which is large and which has rounded edges. See *Designs and Motifs*.

Pinde

Location of manufacture: A nomad tribe in the area of Bukhara.

General description: Similar to other 'Bukhara' rugs, their gul is outlined by the Greek key pattern. Copied today by Pakistan rug-weavers.

Pakistan

For description of antique rugs, see *Indo-Persian*. Modern rugs are not described.

Appendix

Dates on Islamic Rugs

Occasionally rugs bear inscriptions either on the main field or on the border. These inscriptions which are in Arabic may also bear dates which can easily be read. The following are Arabic numerals together with their European equivalents.

Although Arabic writing is written from right to left, arabic numerals are written and read from left to right. A word of caution needs to be injected here, however, as sometimes mirror dates are given, i.e. that is dates written from right to left. It also does not necessarily follow that the date woven into the carpet is the date of manufacture; it may have some other significance.

The date obtained from a rug will be the Hijira date, AH, a date calculated from the date of Mohammed's flight from Medina to Mecca in 622 A.D. The Islamic year is shorter by ten or eleven days in comparison with the Christian. With this in mind, to find the equivalent Christian date first subtract one thirty-third from the AH date and then add 622.

For example, if a rug has an AH date of 1221 its Christian date is calculated as follows. 1221 ÷ 33 = 37; 1221 − 37 = 1184 + 622 = 1806.

Location Maps

CAUCASUS

Caspian Sea

KARABAGH● ●MESHKIN

HERIZ● ●Gorevan

TABRIZ● ●Mehriban

SARAB● ●ARDEBIL

IRAQ

●BIJAR

●SENNEH   ●TEHRAN

●Kerdor ●VERAMIN   ●MESHED

●HAMADAN   ●QUM

●SARUQ

MALAYER●   ●Arak ●KASHAN

●LILIHAN

MUD●

SERABAND●   BIRJAND●

●JOSHAQAN

●Shahr Kord

●ISFAHAN   ●NAIN

●ABADEH

●KERMAN

●SHIRAZ

NIRIZ●

●FARS ●AFSHAR

Kurdistan LURISTAN FERAGHAN MAHAL BAKHTIARI QASHQA'I KHORASAN

Persian Gulf

AFGHANISTAN

IRAN

185

TURKEY (ANATOLIA)

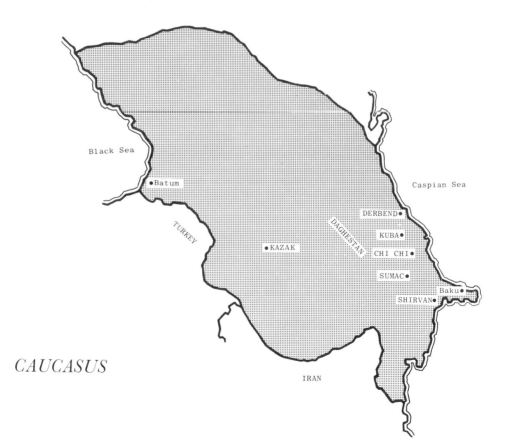

CAUCASUS

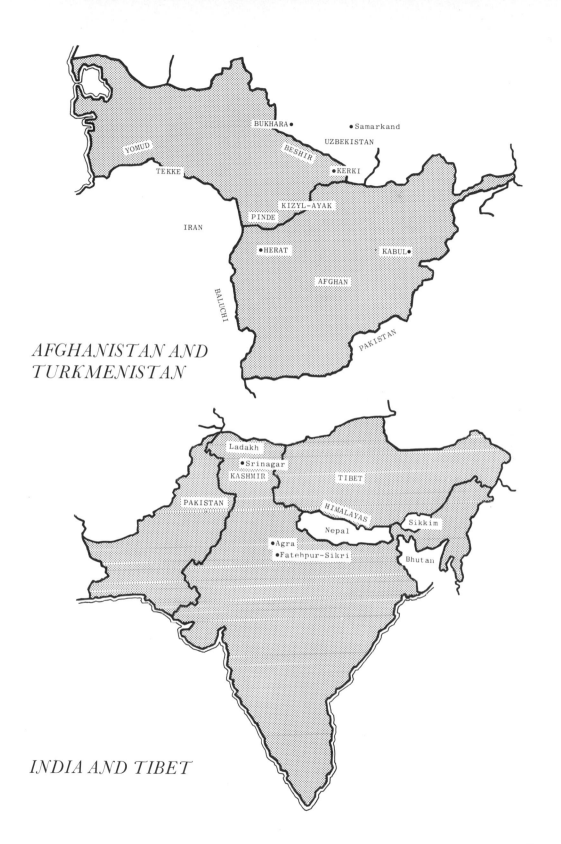

AFGHANISTAN AND
TURKMENISTAN

INDIA AND TIBET

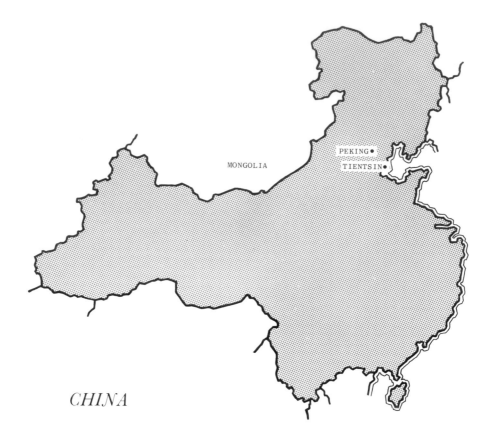

MONGOLIA

PEKING●
TIENTSIN●

CHINA

Examples of Some Rugs and Their Descriptions

A superb 'Star Ushak' carpet dating to the first half of the 17th century. The design consists of octagonal star medallions arranged in staggered rows, alternating with lozenges containing vine tracery, with flowering leafy tendrils contained within a border of interlacing meandering vines.

A 19th century Shirvan rug, the field jewelled with octagons and small geometric motifs around a line of four gabled medallions within a stylised rosette border.

Index

Figures in italics indicate illustrations.